Quantum Politics

BEYOND THE SIMPLE
LEFT-RIGHT
POLITICAL SPECTRUM

Marcus R. Bowman

DEDICATION

To assist the long overdue breaking up
of duopoly power in Washington, D.C.
We haven't even scratched the surface
in our potential for better political outcomes.

CONTENTS

ACKNOWLEDGMENTS

In the words of Justice Ruth Bader Ginsburg, paraphrasing Chief Justice Antonin Scalia, this book attacks ideas, not people. My political viewpoints are certainly close to Justice Scalia and quite conservative; however, in my heart, I also know how much I have chased the truth over the years— challenging myself and reading and listening to every kind of political perspective out there. It is amidst that chase that the ideas for this book were born. For my chase is not entirely unique.
We all are far more independently minded
then our ultimate positions demonstrate.
We *arrive* at our political positions.
With politics, too often people look at each other
for the condition we are in at arrival;
without ever asking about the journey.

1
RADICALLY CHANGING
PERSPECTIVES IN POLITICS

When you consider all the innovations in society and look at the marvels—from Facebook and Netflix to iPhones, spaceships and the Tesla— the question could be asked: And, what of our politics? Bickering on TV, unable to agree on issues such that the government is closing, or might close, and then might re-open. It's time to clean up politics and take our thinking in radically different directions so we can put this sad state of political affairs to rest.

Online political quizzes to tell you where you are politically have questions that sometimes will leave you scratching your head. The few questions they ask feel too narrow, not really getting at your core opinions and views. That, in a nutshell, is what this book is about. Digging deeper into understanding who we are politically. Getting at the fact that our views are far more complex than most any question can get at. And yet we overly simplify our politics to a horizontal line of left to right. We need to up our game in America to have richer discussions and faster, better political results.

We need much deeper analysis into our politics and that will enable new connections and much better solutions. Call it an era of "quantum politics."

In 1844 Ralph Waldo Emerson said[1]:

---

[1] The quote is included in recent books such as *A Country of Vast Designs* (Robert Merry, 2010) and *Hot, Flat and Crowded 2.0* (Thomas Friedman, 2009). Quote online from an 1844 lecture entitled "The Young American" here http://www.bartleby.com/90/0110.html

**America is the country of the future.
It is a country of beginnings, of projects,
of vast designs and expectations.**

Was he ever right about that! And that should be the case for the future. America has always been an innovator—with new ideas and big inventions. But we are losing our ability for dynamic, frank conversations and our country is stagnating in Washington, DC with politicians unable to keep up with the pace of innovation in society; unable even to find basic agreement.

There are 3 main aspects of this book. First, to introduce a new way to look at political alignments—leaping beyond the traditional left-right spectrum, to a "**Political Circle**" which opens our minds to new possibilities. Second, to introduce new ways to understand and categorize individual viewpoints on political issues. This helps to delve into the complexities of each issue such that we understand the depth of nuances to each of our own viewpoints. And hopefully this can improve dialogue and discourse. In other words, it is not always as easy as simply writing someone off because they say they are "pro-life" or "pro-choice." Third, and finally, underscoring the importance of these first two aspects as a foundation for ensuring continued innovation and prosperity in America. We *need* to look at each other differently. We *need* new political alignments. Because we desperately must make bold improvements in America—soon, and radically—if we are going to continue as a free society, and a leader of innovative thought.

We seem to—or should—be heading rapidly to a completely, radically different society. Whether it is flying cars or integrated businesses that cross traditional regulatory lines, we need changes to government that rival those of technology and ingenuity or else we could really stagnate in America.

Where do we start? Washington, DC is in total disfunction. And political dialogue on TV is a circus. Changing our understanding of ourselves and each other is a fundamental element.

**Your political beliefs, my political viewpoints, any of us;
are far more complex than we credit.**

**Our politics do not reside or align along a simple,
straight line somewhere between left and right.**

**Every one of us has nuanced political perspectives
based on unique experiences.**

The "**Political Circle**" is a concept in this book that frames a completely different view of politics that can help to change mindsets and enable the radical changes in both political parties, as well as government, that are necessary for the 21st Century. Not only is this vital to our future but it may end up preserving our own sanity in a nation filled with powerful new technologies that have us all heading 100 miles an hour in every different direction.

The political circle is a shift in mindset. At a minimum, the ends of the left and right are merged together by this circle. The establishment center is not the only meeting place for political agreement. The first thought is how can the far left and the far right come to agreement on anything?

The more important point though is that the "Political Circle" opens up not just a second center, but infinite centers. Any politician, of any politics, has the potential to be a "centrist" of a movement.

A politician needs to find agreement with 51% of the voters. Which expands this circle into yet another concept: that of the cone, or "quantum politics" as I will call it in this book. A skilled politician can put together a coalition of 51% from anywhere along the circle. Find 10% from over there, another 40% right around your viewpoints and a final 1% or more from another point.

As a society we need to break down norms of who it is 'safe' for your favorite politician to talk with. Same goes for each other, and even our political allies. It is not 'selling out' to have conversations—and to seek— solutions. With anyone!

There is a monopolistic-type mentality held by establishment politicians that meeting in the one center and 'rising-above' and agreeing between left- and-right is the only path to agreement.

Changes in political alignments along with technology will facilitate a bold, new future in government.

Radical changes for political parties are likely ahead in the 21st century. Profound changes to our structure of government are also likely this century. Likely… if we really work at it!

A new way of looking at political alignments can help shatter the ongoing stagnation of America and reinvigorate U.S. society to boldly break through to a better future.

Simple changes in political perspective and improvements in political dialogue will set the stage for all of this.

The **Political Circle** is a new way to look at politics. Improving how we can look at each other's different political perspectives. And finding new ways to communicate. Even delving into strategies for having conversations with those that have radically different political viewpoints.

Most importantly, the Political Circle introduces new possibilities for political alignments. It demonstrates ways for new political parties to emerge.

We are not at one end or another. Not one of us is cut off from dialogue with anyone else. We are all much closer to each other—politically—then we are told to think. A left-right political spectrum is as simplistic as a flat earth.

Our individual viewpoints in politics are very complex. So overall, we need to start thinking about politics completely differently.

The United States of America is the greatest country on earth. However, as of early 2018, congressional approval is at 17%.[2] We are successful *despite* our politics, politicians and our government. The U.S. is both a) riding the coattails of prior success and b) driven by the power of ingenuity from so many of millions and millions of hard-working free thinkers across the country. But we are not innovating politically. Imagine if we had all that we have going for us—plus, *plus*, decent politicians—representatives that cared about the people and did not have their own agenda. Representatives not funded by a handful of banks, corporations and billionaires.

The positives that we have in America, I sincerely believe are all in jeopardy if we don't have the same type of innovation and shake-ups in politics and government that we are seeing in the rest of society. We need to think differently. We need to act differently. We need to save this country.

Can technology, social media and the internet catalyze putting it all together to a much better era of politics?

If we play our cards right, very soon, we should see "Yellow States" on our political maps—replacing red and blue. Representing an 'out-with-the-old' stale Republicans and Democrats—yellow for the new independent candidates and third parties that start to win. And in my mind, this means a shattering of the current establishment, banker/corporate dominance. New to me would not be the same characters putting on different hats with flashy Hollywood-style media fan-fare. I am talking, out of nowhere movements—impelling truck drivers and waitresses to Washington, DC—for the big-time stuff, like U.S. Senators. Not people like Scott Brown (what a handpicked name if there ever was one) posing in front of a pickup truck but then becoming the key decisive vote for banker bills. Can the American people decipher the difference? Can enough people start believing they can make a difference going to the polls?

---

[2] http://news.gallup.com/poll/1600/congress-public.aspx

2
TECHNOLOGY
AND… NEW THINKING

Big elections and big changes happened long before modern technology and without social media. In fact, technology might be a hinderance. It has almost been easier to control the population with technology, perhaps deliberately so.[3] Technology however is likely to be a key facilitator. Making new dialogue possible.

Technology and social media are making new connections and faster change possible. Without technology it is not possible. However, new ways of *thinking* are the key element. It will take a combination of these two elements-- new thinking, *and* technology-- to lead us to the better future we need and deserve.

When it comes to elections, major shifts have occurred *without* the help of, say, Facebook and social media. Moreover, it is entirely reasonable to posit that technology is inertia—helping to explain the relative lack of anything different happening in politics for decades. As if technology is even purposely used to hold the people back.[4]

---

[3] https://www.washingtontimes.com/news/2014/jul/18/obey-pentagon-research-indicates-social-media-can-/

[4] There is much that can be read in this area of the impacts of technology on society. For example: http://web.mit.edu/gtmarx/www/techandsocial.html and https://www.technologyreview.com/s/530566/the-impact-of-the-internet-on-society-a-global-perspective/ and https://www.newyorker.com/tech/elements/as-technology-gets-better-will-society-get-worse.

On the road to the bigger structural changes in governing will come fresh perspectives in political alignment and simple dialogue. Much of the structural changes of a so-called "Government 2.0"[5] that are likely to come **will stem out of these far simpler concepts**. Talking to each other. Simply talking to others will help facilitate and determine the structural changes. Talking with those of different political viewpoints. In some ways this could mean less structural changes will be necessary, in another light, it will make bigger structural changes easier.

Therefore, the message of this book is intended to create a mindset and foster an environment that brings people together. One of the ways? Creating space. Creating space in our brains to think completely differently about politics and political alignments.

And creating physical space for people to live the way they want to live. For example, reforming our election process in a way that frees people to vote for the right person regardless of thinking you are wasting a vote. And being free within these 50 united states to have some differences.

Not Going to be Easy.

Any end to the 160+ years (one hundred and sixty years plus) of the grip of power that the Democratic Party and Republican Party have had in Washington DC will be monumental.

We are currently far too politically correct. We should soon witness an awakening of minds that could throw all the caution and political correctness out the window. However, the path forward is not going to be easy. And it is not going to happen the way people might hope or wish. Overall, therefore this book is a caution. It is not likely to be the announced and loud solutions but rather off the beaten path is the way we need to follow. As such, 'things' are more likely to get worse. Potentially much worse. Before they get better.

To fully understand means to shed a lot of preconceptions and notions. What looks bad or sounds bad may actually be part of long-term fixes. For example, the short-term pain of exercising today leads to long-term better health and better shape. And events and news that looks so good today could be masking the real long-term consequences. It may be presented in a flashy way or by a slick professional. Maybe another way of putting this—don't expect to find your answer watching CNN or Fox News. You will just be sinking deeper down the rabbit hole. Slick people pulling the wool over the countries eyes. And those folks have mastered their tactics. They are likely to get better at it before they are seen through.

The future will be led by those able and willing to conduct frank conversations with new and different people than usual. Who? And how?

---

[5] A topic saved for another book.

Who?

Talking and working with people throughout a newly conceptualized political spectrum. Forming partnerships and alignments with people you might not have ever thought you could, or should.

How will all this occur?

Technology impacting politics could be far more revolutionary. In many ways social media will be the facilitator and ultimate conduit for much of the political change. For example, easier dialogue among those in politics will help bring about changes. Social media could be called an indirect technological impact on politics. Direct technology impacts are also possible: revolutionizing how we vote, modernizing the organization and work of government.

However, the bottom line will be thinking differently. Talking with people we aren't traditionally thinking we can, or that we could even get along. And then talking longer. Deeper conversations. Throwing it all on the table until nearly magical, big, pathbreaking ideas and solutions start sprouting up.

3

THE STAKES ARE HIGH

Politically, we have stagnated in America. With so many technological advances and big ideas we need to step up our game—now—to keep delivering on our potential. I believe the stakes are very high.

Our Constitution, as revolutionary as it was, might be becoming old news. Our government—valuable as it is—is too big, too controlling, too bureaucratical, too federal.

Moreover, the political divides in this country are deepening. As such, this book is as much to save the United States of America as anything else. Keeping the U.S. together has not always just happened.[6] Beyond that sensationalistic concern, we desperately need big innovation in politics and governments to keep pace in a global world. We need to start talking about big, controversial issues before we are forced only to react. Do we have the hard conversations and painful discussions that solve our issues and move us forward together? Or do we have the same conversations and figure out a way to agree-to-disagree and live in harmony as separate next-door neighbors? Either way, I believe the key is finding ways that we sit down and make some big-league decisions. No clipping around the margins. Roll up the sleeves. Face reality. And radically transform our ability to achieve higher highs and relieve tension on issues.[7]

---

[6] The early days of possible secession of New England and the debates of Hamilton-Jefferson, to the era of Andrew Jackson such as suppressing revolt in South Carolina, to the Civil War and Presidency of Abraham Lincoln—there have been truly trying times in America's history and we might be far, far closer to such big problems then we are ready to admit.

[7] To me the size of government is one problem. If the President wasn't in

America led the way in the late 1700's paving the way for government *by* the people. The first representative democracy on the planet. Now, *many* countries have followed that lead.

It may be that time again for America. Time to lead the way. 1776 was not small potatoes. It was revolution. It was drastically different government. Now is not a time to be shy.

This time, the stakes might even be higher—a whole world hangs in the balance.[8] The U.S. is the center of so much in the world. In the 1770's the U.S. was (more-or-less) just a gnat for the Kings in Europe to swat about.

Businesses constantly have to stay ahead of the competition. And if the United States wants to remain the world leader. If the United States wants to continue as the best experiment ever in democracy. Then we need to keep working at it. We need to innovate. We need to evolve, adapt and continually improve. And the overriding key is the power of the people. The United States is nothing without its people. We are a unique melting pot. And we need to embrace the healthy aspects of the United States of America and run with them to a better and better future.

What needs to change? With such a low Congressional approval rating we probably should start there. We need a new class of politicians. But how? It has been the same old two parties for so long.

---

charge of so much, and if Washington, DC didn't make so many decisions for the entire country and have so much money to spend, then these elections wouldn't mean as much. To me, get power closer to the people. And reduce the amount of power that any politician has. The point of a good government is to serve the people. Now, we have created a 'winner-takes-all' goliath.

[8] https://youtu.be/5J6jAC6XxAl?t=4m10s

4

TWO PARTY SYSTEM:
THE LOGIC OF TWO PARTIES

The U.S. has pretty much always been a two-party political system.

And, since the 1860's (a long, long, long time ago!) it has been *the same* <u>two</u> political parties.

Why? Why are there only 2 parties?

Is there any logic to a two-party system?

Turns out, yes. There is. In fact, the simplicity of two parties just might could have a correlation to U.S. economic success. How?

The U.S. is a bit unique in having just two political parties.[9] Given the economic and geopolitical success of the United States it is reasonable to posit that simply two parties is a contributing factor.

Logic of Two Party-System?

More parties must be healthier for a truly democratic society! Right? So much talk about the need for a third party and yet none ever develops? For decades and decades—literally over 150 consecutive years—the United States of America has had just two political parties.

Only two ways to vote on an issue:
Either YES, or NO

For every piece of Congressional legislation, it is either a 'yes' vote on that

---

issue or you vote 'no.'[10] In this sense you can really have only 2 coalitions in every vote. You either like the legislation or you don't. With this comes the logic to having only two parties. It gives the people (and lobbyists and otherwise) an idea of where they need to turn. On a particular issue, we have a party that is essentially the 'yes' on that issue and a party that is the 'no' on that issue. Legislation either gets approved or it doesn't. The opposition to a proposed bill knows where they can seek recourse. Therefore, having two parties makes for an effective society. When there is a grievance, one can go to the party in opposition to a certain measure. And only two parties also make it easier to move legislation forward. It is easier to innovate. More efficient.

Arguably, this two-party system could be deemed responsible for the stability in the United States of America as well as potentially linked to economic growth and success.

With decision making in the House of Representatives organized through political parties the U.S. has the advantage of efficient negotiation and disagreement on issues. Also, the two-party system has been beneficial given our 50 states. Each state and its representatives have a narrowed funnel in the two parties for which to coalesce with each other around.

By 1823 even Thomas Jefferson reminisced about a lifetime in politics concluding that two parties made sense. Commenting on Britain:

> "In truth the parties of Whig and Tory
> are those of nature."[11]

Howwwevvvveeerrrr…. right!…. what this does not say is that the two parties that we have today are the *right* parties.

The same two parties? For over 150 years. For one thing, it is definitely a fact, the deck is becoming increasingly stacked against political competition. In state after state it is very difficult for any third party to even get on the ballot. In 2015 I experienced this problem myself realizing it is simply faster, easier, a lot less work and significantly less expensive to register on the ballot as a Republican rather than mount an independent or third party campaign. Beyond getting on the ballot is trying to mount an effective campaign—especially financially… and with a narrow, controlled media—of trying to compete against the Democrats and Republicans.

Thus, we have structural elements that are a major explanation as to why there are only two political parties. That is a problem of these same two

---

[10] Yes, technically three if you abstain and don't log a recorded vote either way.
[11] *The Works of Thomas Jefferson, Volume 12*. 1905. Thomas Jefferson. Pp 323

parties becoming accustomed to their power perch. The incumbents of the two major political parties—Democrats and Republicans—yield their power to pass laws and create regulations that protect them from competition.

A further point is that the results from these same two behemoths is clearly not serving a broad enough swath of the population at large. And two political parties only gives voters two places to turn. Voters have to sacrifice so much of who you are politically to fit into one container or the other. Two political parties do not allow Americans to vote their true values.

Having a third party is not necessarily the answer. However, having different parties is. And having more options is. And looking at the candidates and ourselves differently—no matter whether it stays the same parties—is essential.

Two parties doesn't mean *these* two parties. Two parties doesn't mean the same old two parties. *Why* has it been the same 2 parties for so many years?

5

SAME OLD PARTIES
FOR WAY TOO LONG

Over 160 years. The same two established parties have ruled politics in the United States since the 1850's. The current Republican Party can trace its start back to 1854. The current Democratic Party can trace its origin back to 1840, some say as early as 1828.

The Democratic Party
and
The Republican Party

These two political parties have been the center of United States politics for such a long time that they are institutionalized.

Since the 1860's! Since the time of the Civil War the U.S. has been led by 1 of these 2 parties. Still, statements like this could have sounded as dramatic written 20 years ago. Even the same relevance as much as 50, 75 or 100 years ago the same points could be made.

One could have predicted a change, a new party to emerge, a party shift was coming any time over this long stretch of history and it could have seemed to be eventually inevitable. And yet, here it is early 2018 and nothing has changed.

Why have these two parties stayed relevant and in power for so long?

The Democratic and Republican parties have such a grip on power. Ballot access. Access to deep pockets. That a change might be harder now than ever before.

The grip is so impossibly strong that since the Civil War ended in 1865 no other party (or combination of other parties) besides these two has held

13

more than 7% of the seats in the entire U.S. House of Representatives. In the 1896 election the Populist Party won 22 seats. Not since the 1942 election have even more than 2 out of 435 seats been from another political party! And not even a combination of other parties has held more than 26 seats at once. Since 1865. The grip on power since World War II began however is the most striking statistic and worth repeating.

Since 1942 at least 433 out of 435 seats in the U.S. House of Representatives have been the Democratic Party and the Republican Party. So, at any one time since 1942 no more than 2 seats have been held by a third party or independent.

The Reapportionment Act of 1929 capped the size of the House at 435 (there were temporarily 437 seats in the 86th and 87th Congress from 1959-1963). Since 1945 when World War II ended, there has not been more than 3 members in the House of Representatives that were not a Republican or Democrat. Out of 435 members of the House less than 3 from any other party then Republican or Democrat!

**Over 99% of the seats have been
Republican or Democrat since 1945.**

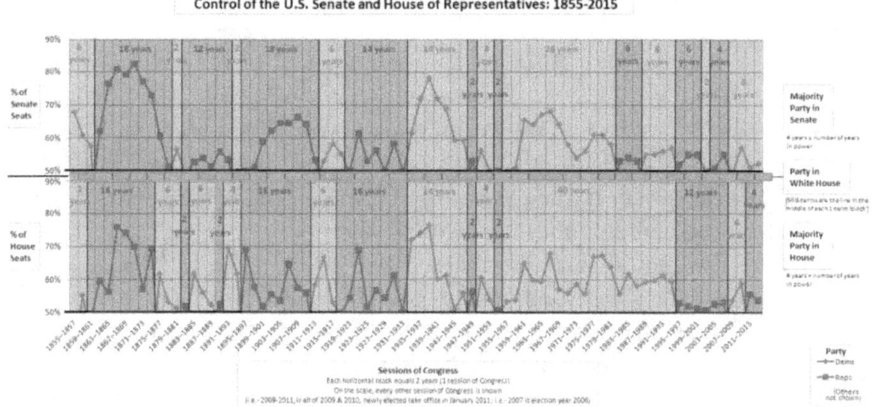

Entrenched Interests

So, with just 2 major political parties for decade after decade after decade what has developed is entrenched interests. The United States desperately needs new energy. Yet the entrenched interests are intent on keeping their power. Largely over the spoils; the amount of money at stake for the winners. The entrenched established interests have created structural road blocks. Ballot access is so difficult for anyone but the major parties. Impossible to see any other way right now. Politicians invested. History with the party. Party is almost first.

The Republicans and Democrats are entrenched parties, dominant machines. Will the parties go global? Has the U.S. figured something out—in having just two political parties—that the rest of the world hasn't? In some respects, as we will point out, you can't argue with the results of a two-party system. Or, as it turns out, the logic of it.

The issue may not necessarily be having only two political parties (though we suspect the future of political alignments over the long-term will be many new political parties and a government structure capable of handling such).

Still the point is stagnation and corruption. Right now, the present political situation—for lack of a better word—has become too established. Stale. Bitter. We throw around terms like 'political establishment'. The term should be used more often. There is far too much consolidated and concentrated political and financial power in the U.S. political government.

Each of the two major parties has entrenched establishments that are working together. We are so established that it has become easy to control and manipulate. All decisions originate out of the same 'center'. Many conclude we really have just one big party. We have found ourselves with a modified two-sided coin in which a flip results in both sides come up heads. In other words, we don't really have two parties. We have two variations of the same mess hall dinner food being served up.

We complain about political correctness as dissent is stifled. Innovative political thought and discourse is discouraged in America of all places, the land of innovation!

Entrenched Perspectives: Voter Apathy

Should there be more than 2 parties for voters to choose between? It is not always only the fault of the political party 'bosses' as there are entrenched *perspectives* among the public. There is also voter apathy. Look at the weak voter turnout. Thus, voters bear some responsibility as well for a fear of the unknown and voting repeatedly not just for the same parties but for the same candidates too. Year after year career politicians are re-elected!

Not since 1968 has any Presidential candidate from a third party won any electoral college votes. A third party presidential candidate has not even won 1 state since 1968. That is nearly 50 years. 11 straight Presidential elections without as much as a dent or even a scratch from a third party or independent presidential bid. Sure, Ross Perot made some waves in 1992. Perot grabbed 18.9% of the vote nationally. Pretty impressive. He didn't win a state though.

Right now, we can all think (and dream) about independent impossible to imagine a United States without Republicans and Democrats. Entire generations of Americans have come and gone, and these two parties are still the only game in town. Dominating Washington DC for about 150 years. Presidential Elections have become classic battles of Bush v Gore (200),

Bush v Kerry (2004); Obama v McCain (2008); Obama v Romney (2012; and now in 2016 Hillary Clinton vs Donald Trump.

Somehow, change *will* come.

What does it take for a new party to form? Seems it's going to take something major. That something major may be as simple as social media. Even with social media it takes a gravitating force and a sea change in perspective. A magnifying character or an insightful new belief. Bold leadership and new ideas are the essential ingredients and social media, or technology is merely a spark and conduit.

6

THE OUTDATED
TRADITIONAL LEFT-RIGHT
POLITICAL SPECTRUM

In the same way there is a relatively simplistic two-party system, our political perspectives are similarly reflected as simply either some degree of left or right.

Conventional wisdom is to categorize voters along a left-to-right line. This is the traditional "political spectrum."

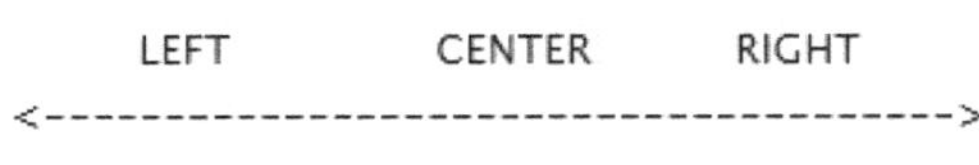

The traditional Political Spectrum

Our political leanings are currently viewed primarily as being placed somewhere along this line. Voters, citizens, people are classified along this line as being either some variation of left, center or a variation of right. You are somewhere on a line. This simple ideological line from the "far left" to the "far right" along this one-line political spectrum.

How did we arrive at this spectrum viewpoint?

Why do we view politics like this?

We talk about the "right wing," and the left. I guess, a bird has two wings, right? An airplane has wings. A left wing. And a right wing.

This spectrum dates back long before the airplane... and even decades

17

before the Democrats and Republicans arrived on the scene. Actually, the late 1700's! The roots of this political perspective reach back to the time of the French Revolution of 1789.

The legislative chambers where the politicians gather to debate and vote. Put yourself in the room.

In the legislative room,
like the politicians gather today—
they gathered (and sat) back then—
next to the colleagues they agreed with.

In late 1700's France, when certain issues came to the forefront, more and more, similar folks started taking up place in the same parts of the room.

There became a usual group on the right side of the room. And an opposing group on the left. You either vote yes or no, right?

In France, on the right, it was supporters of the King. They sat to the King's right. And supporters of the revolution sat to the King's left.

Those who were loyal to the King (King Louis XVI at the time) and religion took their position to the right of the chair.

The manor of gathering in such sides continued past the French Revolution, even as the room was filled with entirely new members when National Assembly was replaced by a "Legislative Assembly." And, again, the same left-right seating arrangements continued when the succeeding National Convention met in 1792.[12]

The characterization and division was thus ingrained. And this notion of a right and left has continued to this day.

> Some believe the identification, and use, of the terms "right wing" and "left wing" is strongest today in France because that is where the concept originated around the 1789 French Revolution based on supporters of the King sitting to his right.

The background is that supporters of the King sitting to the King's right was no accident. Two interesting reasons. First, the Bible references that Jesus was seated to the right-hand of the Father. So, it is entirely likely that was a contributing reason why the supporters of the King were seated to his right. Second, being right-handed was considered normal whereas left-handed was looked down upon for a long time in those days. In both these

---

[12] There would be more changes in the structure of France's legislative branch until 1799 when the existing upper and lower houses of parliament were first established.

cases, the division of sitting to the right vs the left had derogatory perceptions.

The meaning of what "left wing" and "right wing" actually mean has evolved, in some ways substantially, since its original uses in the physical division of groups in the National Assembly meetings in 1790's France. The original distinction in France was based on loyalty to the King and monarchy. The distinction of left-right would evolve into an economic debate much further down the road. For example, Karl Marx book on socialist ideas was much further down the road; his now infamous book *Capital* was published over 70 years later. And left-right can mean different things from one country to the next.

Deja Vu?

The traditional political spectrum is too simplistic.

And, current political analysis is outdated.

A simple left-right political spectrum does not fit reality. We are complex individuals. Every one of us has a difference mix of unique opinions. We have different life experiences. Even if and when we agree on an issue, we are likely to have different reasons why. From one issue to the next our opinions can change. And the degree to which we hold an opinion on this issue or that issue can vary dramatically.

We have been here before.

The earth was flat. For a long time.

Some believe that as late as the time of Christopher Columbus, and even later, that the world consensus remained that of a flat earth.

A flat line political spectrum simply misses the wide reality of our viewpoints and positions. Consider a full range of political ideologies: Social conservative, fiscal conservative, liberal, progressive, libertarian, constitutionalist, environmentalist, anarchist and even include crony capitalists. Where do you fit among these types of labels? How does that transfer to the static, traditional political spectrum line? Then, consider the wide range of different issues: abortion, national defense, government spending, healthcare, education, marriage. Where are you on the line for each individual issue?

You can quickly start to get a picture in your head of how diverse the body of politics can be. The left-right spectrum misses the wide range of alignments that are possible from these diverse subsets.

And it is having consequences.

We need more dialogue. You may get a sense of where someone is on the spectrum relative to one issue—say abortion—and then draw conclusions as to what their positions must be on every other issue. That is where we are missing out. What if, just because someone is staunchly pro-life doesn't mean anything relative to their position on the environment?

We can actually talk about politics with a lot more people than we think.

One key is simply the idea of: Instead of pouncing on the one thing you disagree with, listen long enough and you can find something you do agree on. And from there, more dialogue is possible. Once you find that they agree with you on one thing, their viewpoints on other issues—even if different from you—you might have more tolerance to at least understand where they are coming from.

Our future depends on more dialogue, more listening and more agreeing. Moreover, for us to thrive—for the best innovation—we need new alignments. We *need* a "radical liberal" talking to a "hard-core conservative." Their conversations and dialogue can result both in some political healing but also potentially some really great—and innovative—ideas.

The good news is that a lot of this does happen every day and all day; and all across the country. The media drowns out a lot of the positive. The media makes us believe we are all so far apart. The truth is in our day-to-day life many of us know we are having those conversations and encounters. We only need to believe and have this bubble up to the winning, dominant view.

There has got to be a better way. There has got to be another way of looking at politics.

Today, the earth is a known sphere.[13] A similar revolution in political perspectives will take hold.

---

[13] Or, technically, an ellipsoid https://en.wikipedia.org/wiki/Earth_ellipsoid or "oblate spheroidal" https://en.wikipedia.org/wiki/Earth#Shape. And, well, by the way, ironically a 'flat earth' movement is emerging again! https://en.wikipedia.org/wiki/Modern_flat_Earth_societies

7

THE POLITICAL CIRCLE

The traditional political spectrum aligns each of us as a point on a straight, horizontal line between far left and far right.

The Traditional Political Spectrum

| Far Left | Center | Far Right |
| Liberal | Moderate | Conservative |

People see you, you see others… we look at politicians… as somewhere along this line. This impacts a lot—directly and indirectly (subconsciously)—in terms of who we talk to, who we believe we can talk with, who we believe politicians should work with. In short, its simplicity creates negative tensions, false dichotomies, and most importantly, this line is holding us back.

Bending the line is a first step in reframing our minds to thinking of our political viewpoints beyond the narrow perspective of a simple line.

Now if we place you—your political viewpoints—anywhere along this line, such as on the far left, a key difference is that you can at least 'see' everyone along the curve. There is no longer a wide gulf of people between you and anyone else. Your only divided to the extent you want to be.

Dialogue is perhaps a little more possible. Someone on the far right is no longer separated by millions of people. You can see that person directly. You

21

could, conceivably, make a political connection with them.

The other problem from the simple left-right line is: where is the center? With a right and a left on a line? Right in the middle. Duh. Right? Errr, left. Ok, bad joke. Since we view politics along a left-right line spectrum the center is the middle of the line.

If the line is flexible enough, like a string, then you could keep bending the ends. And the line is bent around until you form a circle. What if we took the traditional spectrum and connected the two ends?

That is the political circle.

The traditional horizontal political left/right line is bent to form a circle. The traditional middle is at the bottom of the circle. Fully bending the line into a circle takes the extreme far left and connects with the extreme far right.

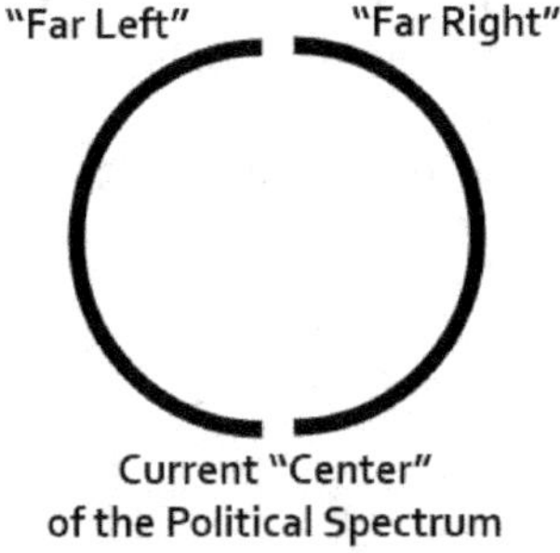

Wrapping the line all the way around seemly creates another center. The political circle. There are two centers so far as we label each of us as part of a dominant party of the left and a dominant party of the right. Spin this circle around 90 degrees.

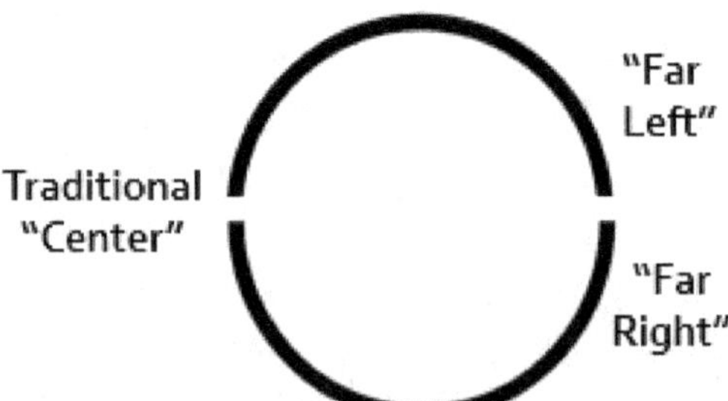

The ultimate result in looking at politics beyond a simple line is that with an updated perspective no one is an "outsider" that is on the "far," "extreme"

of anything. The circle could be spun and positioned any which way.

Political Spectrums placed on a Circle
Everyone has their own personal center.

This could, in part, represent the separation of political parties from the political spectrum. Parties change. People can change.

Conventional wisdom is to wonder how in the world the "extreme views" of right and left could connect in *any* way. As we will get into later, it all depends on what issues we look at.

Anyway, the point here is not for me to try and solve what this means. Rather, simply open the door. Open minds. To new possibilities.

There is an evolving trend in America that will reflect itself in one way or the other. The political circle is a new way to think about the possibilities for new political alignments. This concept can be a total game changer. It frees our political minds to all think differently. And more positively. About the options for finding common ground. With anyone. And building coalitions beyond that.

> A circle is natural in many respects. The earth is round. The sun, the moon. The wheel. A bird's nest is a circle. Igloos and teepees are round. The legendary Catholic native American Black Elk was fascinated by the circle saying, "everything tries to be round" and that "the Power of the World always works in a circle."

Working out deals between the power of the Republican Party and the power of the Democratic Party is not necessarily the center of American political perspectives. Or, more to the point, not the only center. The key is to start understanding that the current center is not what the center always has to be. Beyond this, the center, or *a* center, can be formed anywhere on the political circle.

8
THE ERA OF
QUANTUM POLITICS

The way we look at, talk and analyze politics can be so much deeper. Science has yet to really penetrate political thinking. Many industries have seen big advances in thinking, understanding, practice as well as engineering and technology integration. Politics? Not so much.

Politics needs to leapfrog into relativity and quantum theory.

Quantum mechanics, or "quantum theory" is 20th century physics. And it is filled with seeming contradictions. As John Polkinghorne puts it, quantum theory can determine "a calculable probability…" but "no causes for individual events in the quantum world."[14]

You can be in two places at the same time?

Light behaves sometimes like a wave and sometimes a particle?

By time you measure where an object is, it's no longer where it was by time you are evaluating what you measured?

Big picture implications based on the tiniest particles in the universe?

It is not as simple even as a "political circle" which connects the ends of the traditional left-right line; with one narrow conclusion that perhaps the far right and the far left can find areas of agreement.

Maybe *there is* a hard, fixed line at the point of connecting the circle in which there is very little possibility of agreement between the 'extremes' of far right and far left. Was famed poet William Butler Yeats right to lament that "the center cannot hold."[15]

---

[14] *The Polkinghorne Reader*, John Polkinghorne. 2010. Pp 10-11

[15] http://www.lajuntatribunedemocrat.com/opinion/20180115/mark-l-hopkins-center-cannot-hold

Quantum Politics

Our political viewpoints—individually, and collectively—are as complex as quantum mechanics. There are layers of nuance to each of our own positions that few other people are going to be able to fully understand.

My positions and your positions on issues can be boiled down pretty succinctly, but not fully understood for what they really are. In other words, consider an example in which I may be 'too pro-life' to support a 'pro-life candidate' and you might be 'not pro-life enough' to support that *same* candidate. Both of us pro-life and yet neither of us voting for a pro-life candidate—and for completely different reasons!

**If we can acknowledge these common-sense truths
and contradictions it can free us to identify with
whoever we want to in politics and life.**

It is ok to have different perspectives. It should be expected. Even among those that seem to totally agree, there are different reasons and slightly different degrees.

It is not selling out any of your beliefs to work with someone that has a diametrically opposite viewpoint to yours. Two representatives on complete opposite sides of the political spectrum—and/or opposite sides of the political circle could find agreement. If not on any of 9 issues, maybe on the 10th one. Consider, Representative Gomez on the left marked by the blue person. And, Representative Smith, marked by the red person on the right.

On one key issue. Or even a lot of issues. In some cases, the more you talk, the more you understand each other. You might still be very far apart on issues, but you find a way to at least talk about them. Talk so completely that you are able to carve out new ideas and policies that lots of people might also agree with you on.

Bending the line into a circle is another start in looking at political colleagues, opponents, opposites and extremes in different manners. Connecting the far left to the far right does not mean that is the only new possibility. Rather, there are now **an infinite number of possibilities.**

And, philosophically and morally, the circle eliminates extremes. No individuals should be seen as extreme when it comes to political *ideas.*

Quantum Politics means taking our thought process up a notch. Thinking about politics in more complex ways. Agreement could come from anywhere along the circle. Centers of power could develop in a lot of different ways.

Representative Smith and Representative Gomez have their own centers with large groups of voters that share their perspectives. However, with the current political spectrum mentality society doesn't even start to consider this type of alignment is possible. Moreover, this almost *can't* even happen if they really tried. Due to the way Congress has layered on rules, committees and leadership positions beyond anything ever envisioned by Congress—plus the sad state of our dominant, dinosaur political parties and the roadblocks they set up for alternative agreements.

A coalition could be any grouping along the spectrum getting enough votes of a wide block anywhere on the circle.

If you need 51 votes to pass a bill in the U.S. Senate, it does not have to be all Republicans or all Democrats or even help from the traditional center. A quantum perspective of politics is that a grouping of 26 votes from anywhere on one side could be grouped with 25 votes on the other side.

In the image above, the 1 Republican and 1 Democrat that are on opposite sides of the spectrum talk and make an agreement that they take back to the people around them. So, the winning coalition that results in the diagram above has 2 separate elements. One element from the right side of the circle and another element from the left. Call it the bottom-right quadrant and top-left quadrants aligning together to form the 51+, or 217 (50% plus one) necessary to pass the bill in the U.S. House of Representatives. If only such dialogue were possible, as current rules in the House and Senate have evolved beyond the Constitution to route all legislation through leadership silos. Sigh… ok, back to quantum politics…

From there, you can, as they like to say—whip your votes together from literally anywhere along the circle.

You could put your 50% together anywhere. You could take 20% from the top left of the circle and 25% from the bottom right, and piece together another 6% to get 51. Forming a coalition randomly of anyone along the circle is possible—literally pulling together people from any political persuasion.

Bending the traditional political spectrum into a circle, this enables any of us to pick from along the circle from various points here and there. Creating a consensus without necessarily being a party. A few representatives from here, some others from over there, etc. You have a consensus/majority to move an agenda forward. There are so many possibilities.

The straight line really narrows our collective mindset about who might be a political ally, or friend. Perhaps, cynically, even deliberately so now.

Cylinder

Like the contradictory aspects of quantum mechanics, the point of these ideas and illustrations is simply to expand our minds. To think way outside the box. We can take the circle. And put it up on its side. And add cylinders to each end.

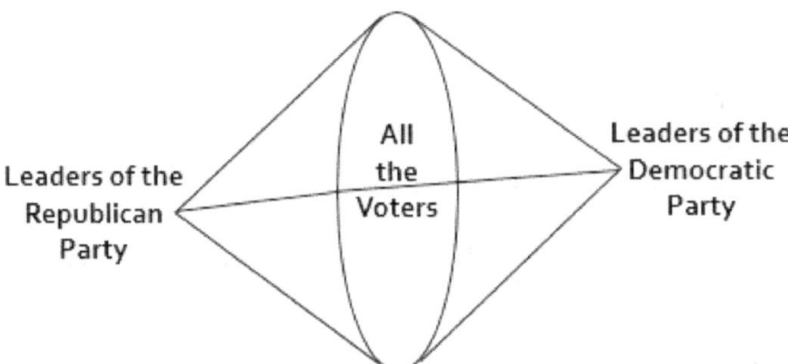

The leadership of any political party is not that many people. This diagram above presents a different way of looking at party leadership. Or any leaders, really. Good or bad, the best leaders or not, the point is that they are outside the circle connecting to it like any person would. They are not a part of some "moderate," "centrist" higher ground. The only higher ground is doing the right thing.

Forming coalitions in a circle. Can be from any points. It's the skill of the individual pulling a coalition together.

Below is another way to flip the cylinder to illustrate the point of being able to work across the entire political circle—tapping people from anywhere on the spectrum of political viewpoints.

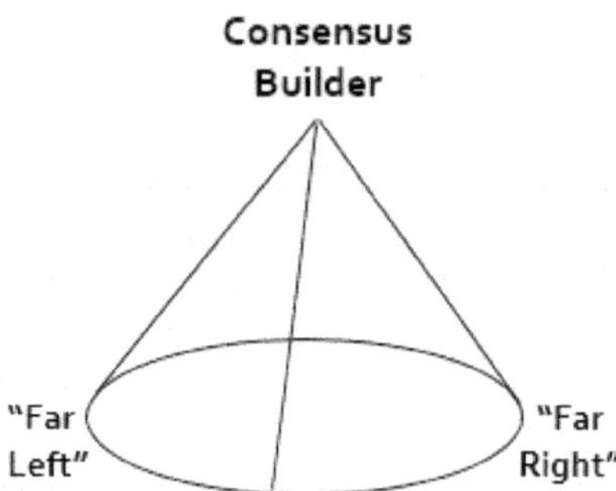

This puts a person at a point where they can see how they can become a facilitator—and leader—to get things done politically, connecting to people anywhere along the circle. The point here, again, is only to put a mental image in your head of possibilities.

In this way, the person is not working out of where they, themselves, are pigeon-holed on the circle. Rather, this person is liberated to approach anyone. Not for who they are believed to be but as a "new person" so to speak. For one, and all issues? Establishing oneself independently as someone that can talk to anyone. The freedom to view anyone as a potential ally.

And, with that, the diagram is not only for a consensus builder, but for you. Yes, you. You can choose to see everyone out there in a different and better light. And see yourself as that person. A) no longer are you yourself somewhere on the line (and potentially directly or indirectly personally limited for what you believe you can do), but B) you can also see every single person out there as a potential *direct* connection politically.

A coalition can come from anywhere. It is a matter of leadership and size of your tent. It does not have to be a contiguous coalition. It is much deeper than that.

3D Three Dimensional

Three-dimensional space (or "3-space") requires three values to determine its position. In other words, a third axis (shown in the diagram below) beyond the typical horizontal and vertical, or x and y axis. This Euclidean space is illustrated graphically with a z-axis added to x and y.

It is like trying to create a three-dimensional chart/diagram in Microsoft

Excel. It taxes our minds and the computer's abilities. Even if we can create the diagram it is hard to interpret (such as below).

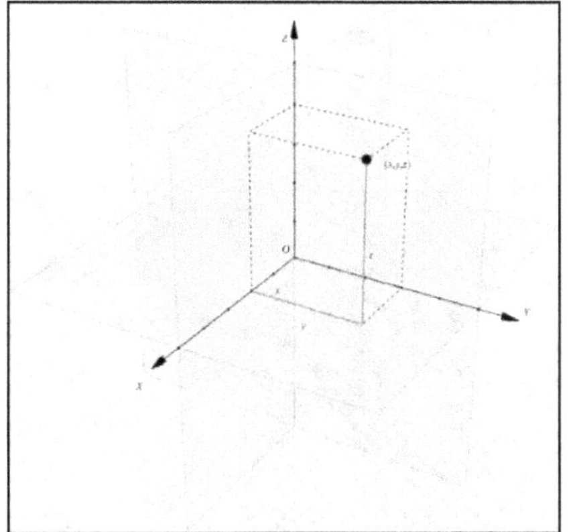

Euclidean space illustration of 3 dimensions.[16]

Consider an odd-shaped package too. There is the length of the box. Then there is the width of the box. And its height. And even beyond those three you have the "girth." Consider girth as the number representing "wrapping around" the package.[17] A so-called "Tensor Diagram" demonstrates the functional mathematics involved in determining girth. Shown here below merely to, as I like to say, open minds to what is possible in political analysis. And not so much even actual mathematical analysis, but in terms of looking at, and understanding, each other's politics. That we are each far more complex than "liberal" versus "conservative." Our current politics doesn't even scratch the surface of our collective potential.

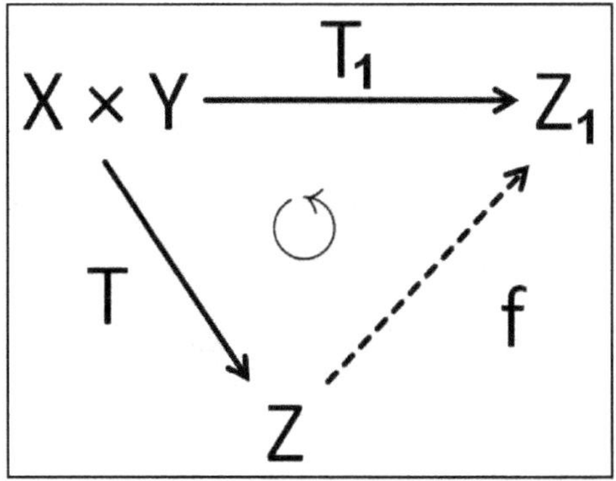

"Tensor Diagram" in description of "Girth" as a matter of Banach space.[18]

If you take a sphere (round global circle) and turn it into a three-dimensional object you actually have what is known as a "2-sphere." To get a "3-sphere" becomes a "glome" or hypersphere with incredible complexities as illustrated below.

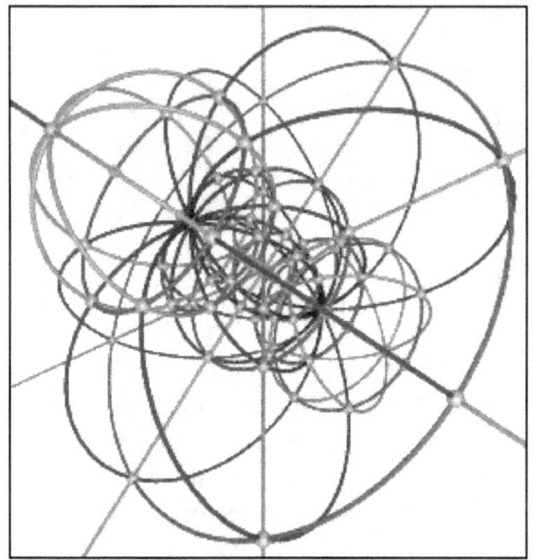

3-Sphere (glome/hypershere)[19]

This is the level of complexity we should be thinking when talking with someone about politics. Not so simple to pigeon-hole anyone. Give some credit for differences.

We will delve toward these levels of complexity as we try to illustrate the true realities of our own political viewpoints.

The political circle demonstrates that each and every one of us is part of a fluid, contiguous line—with "access" (so to speak) to be in the center of pulling people together just as a "moderate" "centrist" does.

It takes one issue to agree. The world does not necessarily need to be reinvented for massive, revolutionary political change. The biggest changes in 20th century physics came at the simplest measure of the universe.

Relevant Aspects of Quantum Mechanics to Politics

Here are examples of relevant aspects of quantum theory to politics.

---

[18] Per Wikipedia: https://en.wikipedia.org/wiki/Banach_space and https://en.wikipedia.org/wiki/Banach_space#/media/File:Tensor-diagramB.jpg.
[19] Per Wikipedia via https://en.wikipedia.org/wiki/3-sphere and https://en.wikipedia.org/wiki/3-sphere#/media/File:Hypersphere_coord.PNG.

- Chaos theory (a butterfly flaps its wings in China and a rain storm results in California): it only takes one conversation, one relationship to start a huge, enormous change.
- Light as a particle and/or a wave: people not only hold contradictory opinions from one issue to the next, but even their viewpoints within what would appear to be only one political issue are far more complex—not so easy to pin down, and even on one narrow aspect of an issue a person may have some back-and-forth nuanced differences.

A contradiction in politics is that it takes only one issue to find some agreement while at the same time the complexity of so many issues and so many people has to be even remotely understood. Say what? Exactly the point.

How do we turn this new… umm… energy… into something bigger and lasting?

We need to better understand each other. For one thing, through improved dialogue. Or beyond improved dialogue, just trying some dialogue in the first place! And, also looking at ourselves and others. Understanding our politics at a much deeper level. That your neighbor must be a total liberal, defined by information gathered on one issue based on one question does not begin to scratch the surface of complexities there. We need better ways of classifying who we are politically. And in determining how to make those classifications we will find out that we will start to view everyone in a lot more nuanced way. More appropriate and fitting ways.

9

UNIQUE INDIVIDUALS: COMPLEX AND NUANCED DIFFERENCES

Politics is far more complex than societal conventional wisdom.

On an individual level politics is complex.

We all have our independent views.

Each of us might have strongly held opinions.

And, they could change. Moreover, the answers we give to a question could even be intentionally vague or evasive.[20]

Why do we hold the positions we hold?

If I am "pro-life" or "pro-choice" what does that mean?

It seems like a simple question; yet for this controversial issue, and really any political question, our individual viewpoints are far more complex than we give credit. And questions like this are often far too broad to mean as much as they could or should. There is a lot more to our politics than just the answer to a question.

Like a 'yes' or 'no' question you pick one: pro-life or pro-choice.

If a person, Sam, is "pro-life," how "pro-life" are they?

If Sam is "very strongly" pro-life how much does it impact his (or her) voting? Does the issue of abortion always impact his voting?

What are the solutions to the "pro-life" issue? How many of them would Sam support? Does he say he is "pro-life" because (generally speaking) he is,

---

[20] For example, people are not always going to say who they really support and/or who they really voted for. Politics can be close to home. Neighbors, family members, friends and co-workers could all be among the reasons why you might not want others to know why and for who you voted.

but has his one lines in the sand (so to speak) of where he believes abortion is the only option?

If you are "pro-choice" many of those same questions. And, where do you draw the line on various legislative proposals that come up. As an example, someone might be "pro-choice" but not be supportive of abortion after 10 weeks, or 20 weeks, or the last trimester. They might even be *adamantly* pro-choice, but have a strict, specific time limit when they believe the baby is 'viable' and abortion should be avoided, or not permitted.

There is so much analysis that could be done into our positions and why we vote and who we vote for. And, what would we decide if we were in Congress? On this issue, or that specific piece of legislation.

And what about one issue to the next? When we don't have a job, the economy sure rises to the top of our concerns. Whereas in peace and economic security, we might have personal/moral/social issues that are our most important considerations.

The degree, or intensity, of our support for a particular issue can change. Your sister has a child. And you see the beauty of that tiny baby and your thoughts about pro-life/pro-choice are impacted, either completely or just in a minor way. The point, we are products of our own unique experiences.

How do we determine our viewpoint?
Unique personal reasons… and experiences.

When it comes to a particular election, or vote in Congress, we may form opinions based on a wide variety of things. Some of us are exposed to more, or less, information. Circumstances of what we hear, read, see, talk about with others—all of it is unique to us individually.

If you recognize
any of this about yourself,
it is time for us to recognize
the complexity of politics
for every other one of us.

We all approach politics a little differently. This is our level of care or concern. We all bring different experiences to why we hold the views we do. This is how we were brought up, who we talk to and what happened to us along the way. Issue be issue we are different. The number of dimensions to analyze in truly breaking down the political climate is at a minimum three:

1. Your stance (yes or no)
2. The hardness of your stance (scale of 0 to 10)
3. The importance of that issue relative to other issues.

10
ISSUE-BY-ISSUE:
MULTIPLE LAYERS OF COMPLEXITY TO POLITICAL VIEWPOINTS

When it comes to a particular political issue, a simple 'yes' or 'no' really tells very little about a person or their politics. Especially depending on how the question itself is worded!

Taking a step beyond, what is the scale and degree to your level of support (below, left)? Beyond, 'yes' or 'no' to a weighting.

What is your level of support for the issue '0-to-10'?

For example, how 'pro-choice' are you? From, say, 0 (low support) to 10 (strong support)?

Second (below, right), how important is the issue to you? Such as deciding whether or not you will vote and/or degree of impact on affecting your decision who you will be voting for.

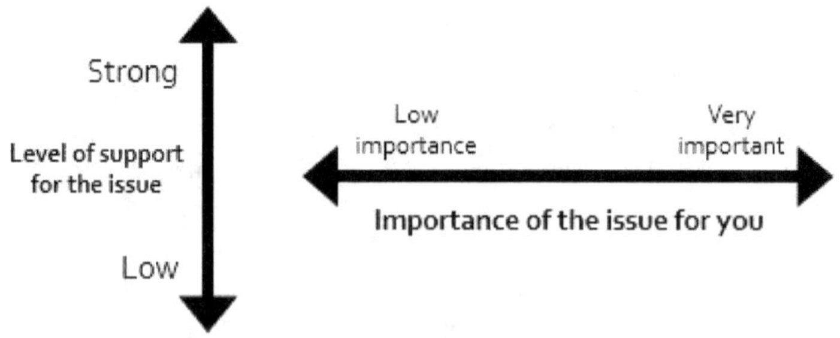

One: Degree of Support for an Issue

People support or oppose issues in matters of degree.

If asked 'yes' or 'no' about an issue you could quickly answer one way or the other and the person could have a whole wide range of conclusions to draw. Are we too quick a lot of times to form opinions without really understanding the true position other people have? 'Yes' or 'no' gives another person no idea what your degree of yes is. Is it a 100% yes? Is it a 50% yes?

Take one issue. It can be posed as a 'yes or no' question. Do you agree or disagree? People that agree on an issue though could have entirely different degrees of support.

How strong is that viewpoint on a scale of 1 to 10?

When describing how important are national security and defense spending your viewpoints are: on a scale of 1-10 from 'not worried about national security and more defense spending' (1) to 'very concerned, more defense spending is needed (10). What would you answer? On that scale of 1 to 10, *how much* do you agree or disagree? Two people, Barack and Donald both answer 'yes' that defense spending is important. Donald, *for example*, however is a 10 for *how much* he agrees while Barack says, *for example*, 6.

Two: Importance of that Issue

Next, how important is that issue to you?

Does it drive you to the polls? Is it the first question you ask about a politician? How much does that issue influence your voting decisions?

And, how important is that issue relative to other issues? Do you have a handful of issues that are equally important? Or does one issue really define your politics?

We are all very different!

On relative issues, you might be a "10" on the scale in *support* of pro-choice; however, in the vast range of issues (from economic growth to national defense spending to our federal deficit and gay marriage) pro-choice could rank lower than a lot of other issues. When asked on a scale of 1 to 10 whether you *vote* based on 'pro-life' issues you might answer 2. So, the issue is not that important to you from a voting standpoint.

One, how much does that issue influence your voting decisions?

Two, how important is that issue relative to other issues?

Are you always that way about the issue? Some people are hardline "pro-choice" for women's freedom of their own body. Others are hardline pro-life focusing on a baby's life is involved. For both of these "hardliners" this issue is more important than every issue.

Others could have similar overall feelings about the issue; however, based on whatever else might be affecting them, the importance of the issue is going to vary year-to-year. For example, if you don't have a good job you might be thinking first and foremost about the economy when assessing candidates.

Some people might analyze every last difference in a candidate's remarks to make a decision based entirely on one issue. While others will listen in a more abstract manner and might not see that much of a difference between two candidates on an issue of importance and thus move down the list to another issue in differentiating a candidate. In other words, pro-life or pro-choice is their most important issue but in a certain election of two candidates that issue is off the table and all other issues are what they base a decision on. Or they decide not to vote because the one issue they care about they can't seem to deduct a difference and so they don't think it matters.

What do you mean by important?

The point is… wow. It's not at all simple!

Looking at both these dynamics in a chart

The next step is evaluating these two criteria together. For example, someone could be extremely pro-choice but just not that interested in the politics of it; whereas another person is just as 'pro-choice,' *and* they base their entire decision about which candidate to vote for only on this issue. Two ways to organize this information shown below.

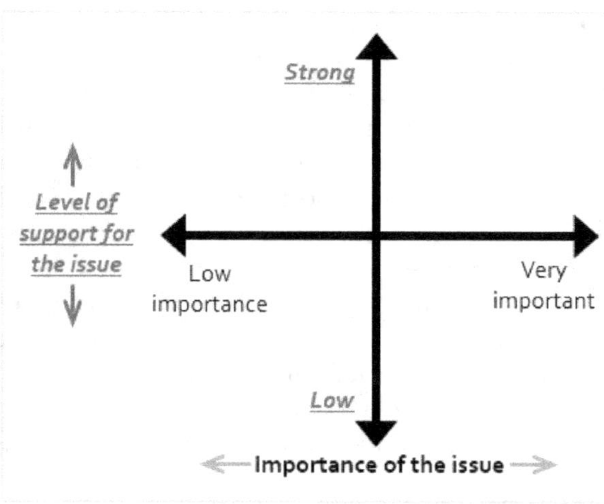

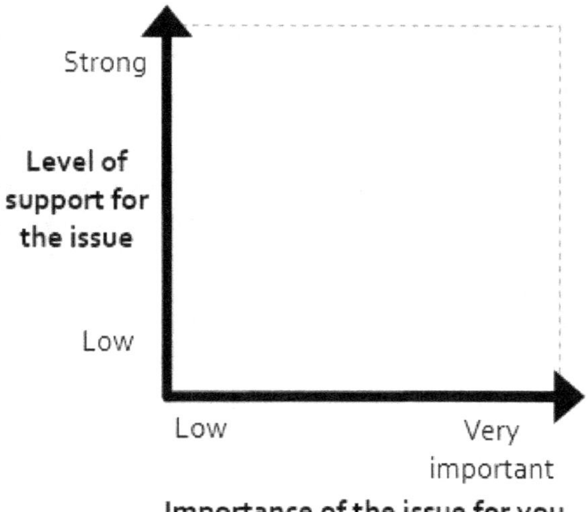

Vertical axis. What is your stance on the issue? How much do you support the topic or oppose? At the top, you would strongly support the issue as framed. At the bottom you would be adamantly opposed. In the middle you could maybe care less about the issue.

Horizontal axis. How important is the issue? From left to right. Not being important at the far left of the spectrum and the issue being of utmost importance to you on the right.

Next, below, using the first matrix we place a hypothetical individuals' viewpoints on the "Pro-Choice" issue (marked by green dot). The person has a) very low support for 'pro-choice;' so, in other words, they are 'pro-life.' And, b) places high importance on the issue. Thus, the person likely decides to go vote and chooses who they will vote for based on this issue.

Political Issue: Pro Choice

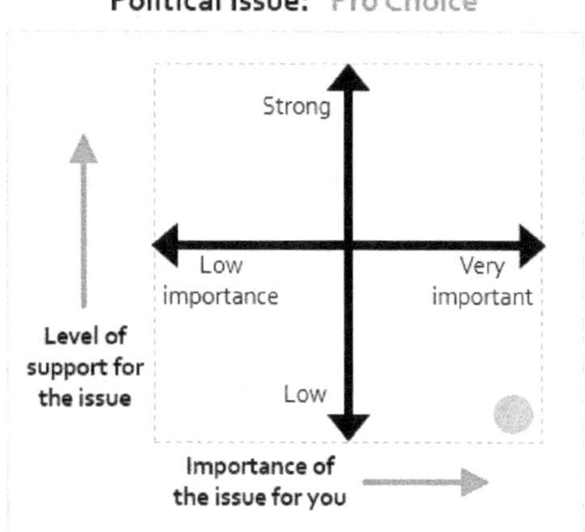

On an individual-to-individual level this type of graphic can be a starting point to help understand where each other are coming from. And for politicians, analysts and policy-makers, placing a bunch of dots representing, say, 100 different people's views could paint an interesting picture, and even be scored.

Conversely, shown below (using the graph), another person could also be 'pro-life' (green dot marking the individual's viewpoints). However, this time the issue is not as important. This person has a deep personal conviction for 'pro-life.' However, it seems this person does not base their voting decisions on it. An example, could be someone that believes they align with Democrats on more of the issues. Therefore, when it comes to the issue of 'pro-life' they turn the other way, in effect. They do not let this position affect how they look at the Democratic candidate.[21]

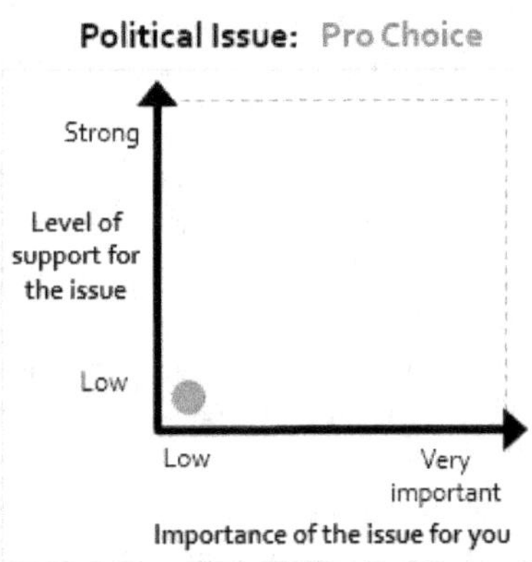

Without going into too much more detail each issue is itself far more complex than a topical question. In other words, the more specific the question is. Do you support late-term abortions? Do you support an abortion at 20 weeks? Those questions get to greater levels of detail and as such with any issue: defense spending. Do you support defense spending? Do you support spending on a certain new aircraft project? Do you support this or that war front?

Moreover, the precise wording of a question can have a huge impact on people's answers.

How the question is worded
And even what questions are asked
(and what questions are not asked)
Impacts answers, Impacts Results

---

[21] Presuming the Dem candidate is following the Party pro-choice platform.

11
CHARTING OUR POLITICS

How do we classify our political viewpoints? Currently, poll questions are one way. People are asked if they are liberal or conservative, Republican or Democrat. "Exit polls" from voters leaving the polling place gather info on different political issues. And surveys ask viewpoints on various issues.

ISideWIth.com and TheAdvocates.com have surveys online.[22] They are a relatively recent, very positive step in the right direction of trying to build understanding of the depth of our political opinions and differences.

"Nolan charts"[23] is the general term given to how the results of these type of surveys are presented. The Nolan chart is among the earliest efforts to look at our political perspectives on two axes.[24]

First, below is a results matrix from the online quiz used by Advocates for Self-Government.[25] A short survey generates a score; and a dot is placed within the diagram to reflect your positions on the issue. The quiz differentiates mainly between "personal issues" (social issues) and "economic

---

[22] Some of these online surveys it is unclear whether there is an agenda behind them. The wording of survey questions can have a huge impact on what the results are.

[23] Named after David Nolan who helped start the Libertarian Party.

[24] Survey data research conducted by Hans Eysenck in the 1950's is credited with developing this method.
https://en.wikipedia.org/wiki/Nolan_Chart#Development

[25] To some extent, the results would need to be taken with a grain of salt due to the name of the organization and potential that they hope people see themselves as "advocates for self-government."
https://www.theadvocates.org/quiz/quiz.html

issues" left-to-right. And then also differentiates "libertarian" from "statist" top-to-bottom. The latter distinction I find quite beneficial—in other words, do you like when the government is deciding issues and involved more in managing society; or would you prefer more individual and business freedom?

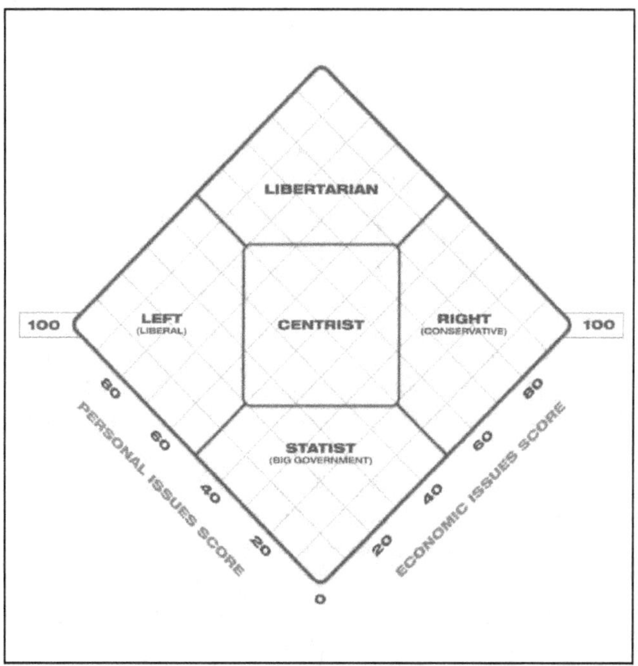

Via Advocates for Self-Government[26] Quiz questions.[27]

---

[26] https://www.theadvocates.org/quiz/reprint-and-copyright/

[27] Described on their website as the "smallest political quiz," the quiz seeks an answer of either "agree," "maybe," or "disagree" to the following ten questions (first five on "personal issues" and last five on "economic issues":

1. Government should not censor speech, press, media, or internet.
2. Military service should be voluntary. There should be no draft.
3. There should be no laws regarding sex for consenting adults.
4. Repeal laws prohibiting adult possession and use of drugs.
5. There should be no National ID card.
6. End "corporate welfare." No government handouts to business.
7. End government barriers to international free trade.
8. Let people control their own retirement; privatize Social Security.
9. Replace government welfare with private charity.
10. Cut taxes and government spending by 50% or more.

Next, here is the matrix used by ISideWith to categorize voters:

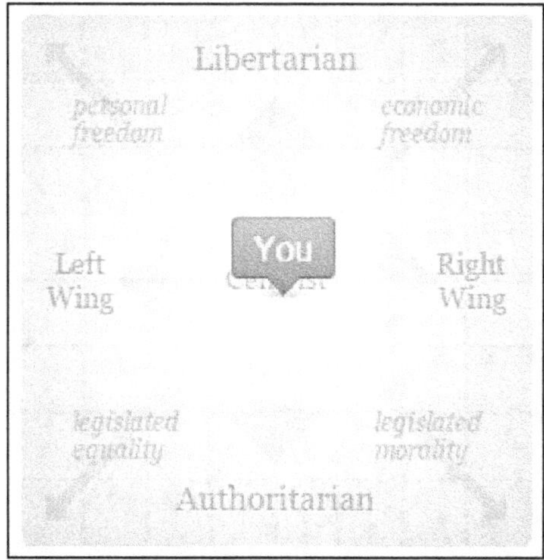

This chart is used at ISideWith.com[28]

In addition to the dichotomies of "left wing – right wing" and "authoritarian" (statist) to "libertarian" the ISideWith matrix differentiates "personal freedom vs legislated morality" and "legislated equality vs economic freedom." Truly insightful attempts to take the conversation up a level, so to speak. However, just what type of framing is this? What is the definition of "legislated morality" and "personal freedom?" A liberal framing of questions presumes moral authority. Therefore, having a conservative viewpoint on a social issue is viewed as "legislating morality" whereas the "left wing" on social issues is being given credit for being for "personal freedom."[29] Even economic freedom gets very complex. Do you support mega corporations and big, national banks or do you support local, small businesses?

Anyway, these types of surveys are great. And they help position you in a deeper manner. However, so much is missing.

---

[28] Actual source of image http://i.imgur.com/F1qrGRc.png as used on the website ISideWith http://www.isidewith.com/

[29] As examples, liberals are not ok with a business owner deciding whether they want to bake a cake or not. Liberals want to "legislate morality" in that case. Same with the case for "gay marriage" and legalized abortion. Liberals want government decisions and laws for these moral positions.

12
CATEGORIZING AND STACKING MULTIPLE ISSUES

How can we start to stack up our positions on more than one issue? And, formulate results that mean more, or illustrate the complexity of our opinions across multiple issues?

The Nolan Chart more-or-less tells you what you already know. And, depending on the questions (and wording of the questions) paints a picture slightly in the direction of what the host of the poll wants you to think. For example, you take the poll at the libertarian website and voila, you are deemed a little bit more libertarian than you thought you were.

More than any of this, the charts are a little bit of a black box. Why do they pick the 10 or so questions that they do? And how are they weighting the questions and adding up the result?

Finally, what are any of us learning—usefully—from these survey results?

To address, or solve, these questions—the task for the future is two-fold. One, to simplify the information we are gathering. Make the questions fully transparent. Make the calculated results meaningful, and understandable. Second—at the same time—step it up a bit. Generate some numbers. Plug a bunch of people in the results. Let's start learning something.

The chart below, we look at 3 issues at the same time: abortion, gun control and gay marriage. Opposing any of these is a conservative/right-leaning position. Supporting any of these is left-leaning/liberal. So, the issues are plotted on the chart from left-to-right based on the degree of your support or opposition. In this first chart below, the individual, call him Mitchell, is decidedly left of center on all these issues.

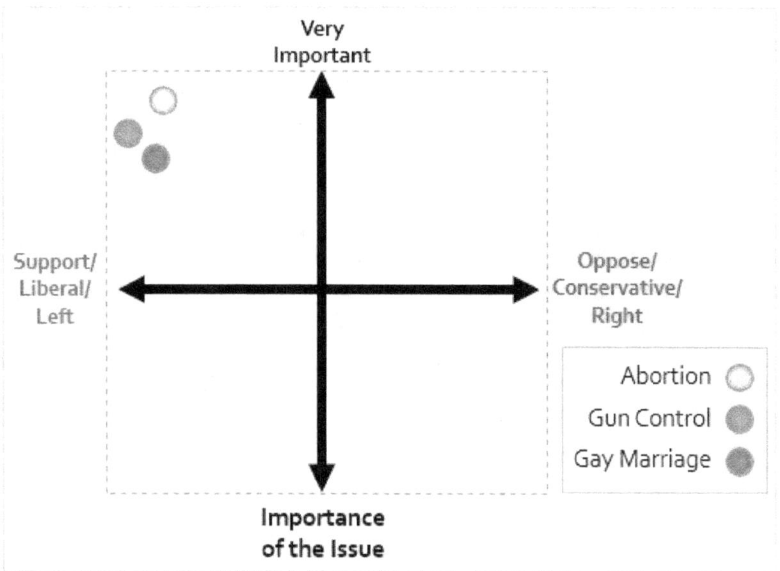

The next example looks at these same three issues from the perspective of a different hypothetical voter, call her Samantha.

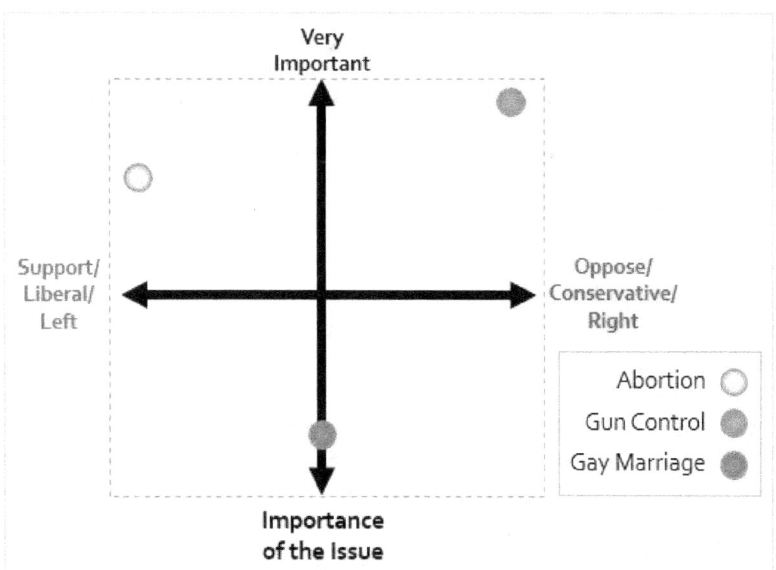

On this second one, let's see. No opinion on gay marriage. Not for it. Not against it. Doesn't really care about the issue at all. Gun control? Totally against gun control. Hunter? Wife of a hunter? Daughter of a hunter? Pro-choice. Supports abortion. Pretty strongly.

Things get a little complicated with Samantha. How do we label her? Is she a centrist? A moderate? Because a liberal issue and conservative issue cancel each other out? She is conservative on some issues, liberal on others. But she is hardline conservative on gun rights. And hardline liberal on abortion rights.

How is Samantha going to vote? Starts to get harder to say right? In this case, the _relative importance between the issues_ of "gun control" versus "abortion rights" is likely to decide her vote. It would vary race-by-race. For example, if two candidates were relatively the same on their gun control positions Samantha might decide based on her pro-choice stance. Or, vice versa.

The charts above seem more simplistic than the Nolan Chart. However, they provide a lot more detail. Actionable information so to speak.

Then, of course, there are a lot more issues that could be added in.

Below, another way to look multiple issues at once. Stacking. Including a few more issues.

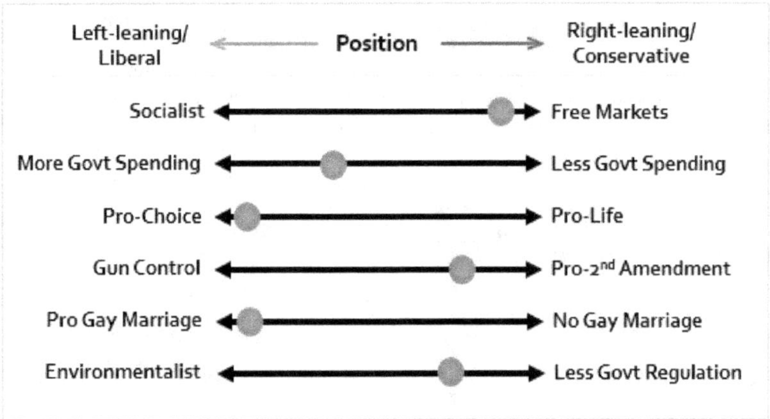

Positions of another hypothetical voter, Bill, on 6 different issues. Bill's positions fixed for each issue by a green dot spanning left to right between a liberal and conservative position.

A couple observations. First, any of these issues are more complex than an overarching label, such as "environmentalist," "socialist," or the opposite of "environmentalist" being defined here as "less government regulation."

To get useful results, the questions need to be more precise. Nevertheless, this helps advance the discussion. Another way to help highlight people's differences. While not as succinct as cranking out one result like the Nolan Chart, this type of stacking helps another person to really understand more about Bill and his politics. This illustration, stacking issues, shows several positions whereby you can truly learn something about Bill.

Let's look at another hypothetical voter, Tony. Tony's views, stacked below, clearly jump off the page as a total liberal. Plotted on a Nolan Chart, for example, there probably wouldn't be any doubt.

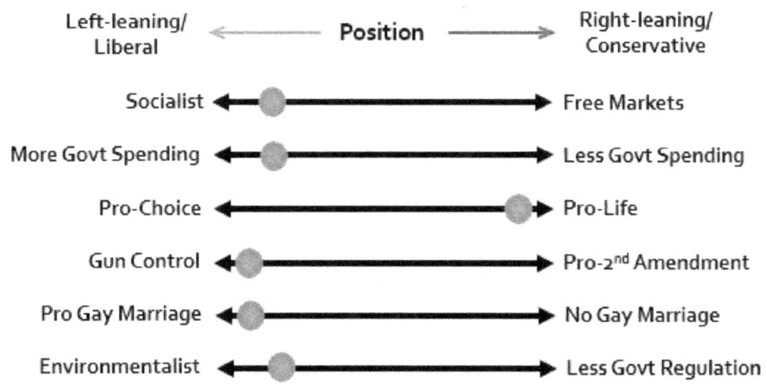

But what happens when *you* meet Tony? What if the first question you ask is "Are you pro-choice?" What will you think of Tony then?

What if you talk to Tony about all the other issues besides abortion.

Imagine, first, a conservative talking with Tony. And on all the issues they find Tony to be a total liberal over and over. They walk away before touching on abortion and never learn there was at least one agreement. These types of diagrams can help us think about making less assumptions about people's politics.

Now consider a liberal (on every single issue) talking with Tony. Once they find out Tony is "pro-life" they start to wonder about him. Is Tony truly liberal? Will Tony sell out the entire liberal agenda? If Tony is "pro-life" is he *really* as pro-gay marriage? Are his positions on all the others sincere?

These are tendencies all of us seem to have when it comes to even people we agree with. If we detect *any* difference it makes us question the totality.

The chart above is the real world. We are all different. Sometimes very different. Sometimes a little bit different. Sometimes even tiny nuances amount to big overall political differences. We can step back and look at it all the other way.

Mostly different = Sometimes the same

Mostly the same = Sometimes different

Conservative? Don't expect that every conservative is conservative the way that you are? Your most important issue might be abortion. Their most important issue could be lower government regulations.

Liberal? Don't expect that every liberal feels all the issues in the same way you do. One is very concerned about the environment. Another is most passionate about gun control. Life experiences are an element.

Our politics are complex. Our individual viewpoints are sometimes a lot more nuanced than we can convey.

On an individual basis, the myriad of different issues illustrates the complexity in trying to pigeon-hole what our viewpoints are.

13
RANKING ISSUES AND
SCORING OUR POLITICS

Adding up and analyzing where we stand politically based on the combination of several different issues can be very beneficial. Here are a couple new examples. Six different issues.

This time including comprehensive scoring; and illustrating how they rank the relative importance of the different issues.

These are different people, issues and stances then the examples from the previous chapter. The diagram below asks for a weighting from -100 (strongest support of the left-leaning position) to +100 (strongest support of the right-leaning position) with 0 marking a balanced view on the issue.

First, Jessie. Her positions on the issues are clearly more left-leaning. Several of the issues she takes very passionately liberal positions.

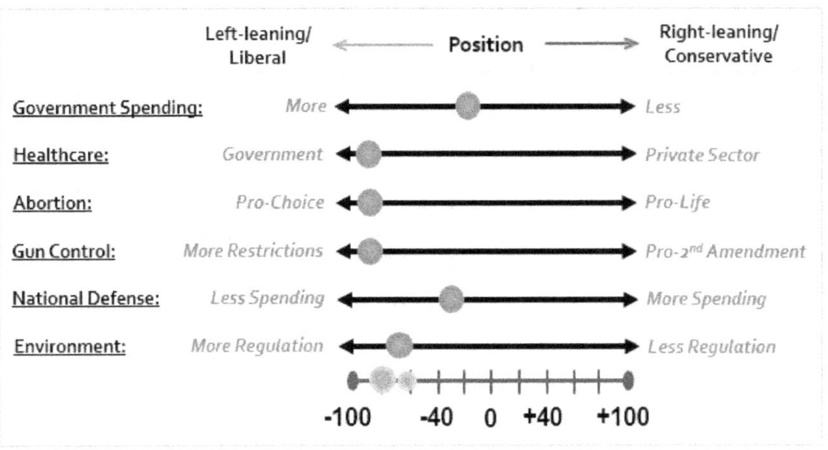

Below, is a table showing the data. Scoring these issues with the same importance, Jessie averages a -63.0 (first column). Fairly liberal. She has relatively moderate views on government spending and national defense which balance out her more strongly held views on social issues.

The second column in the table below shows the weighting Jessie assigns each issue. The amount of government spending and spending on national defense—both of those issues don't matter as much to her (weighted only 5% each). Healthcare and abortion are her top issues (both weighted 30%). Because her more moderate positions are issues she also doesn't care much about when her issue rankings are considered, Jessie's weighted score comes up as -80.0. Even more liberal/left-leaning than the chart above illustrates.

Issue	Position	Ranking
Government Spending	-10	5%
Healthcare	-90	30%
Abortion	-90	30%
Gun Control	-90	15%
National Defense	-30	5%
Environment	-70	15%
SCORE	-63.3	-80.0

Next, below, Martin. His views are a little more complicated. He has a very conservative opinion on the 2nd Amendment while having a very liberal opinion with respect to healthcare.

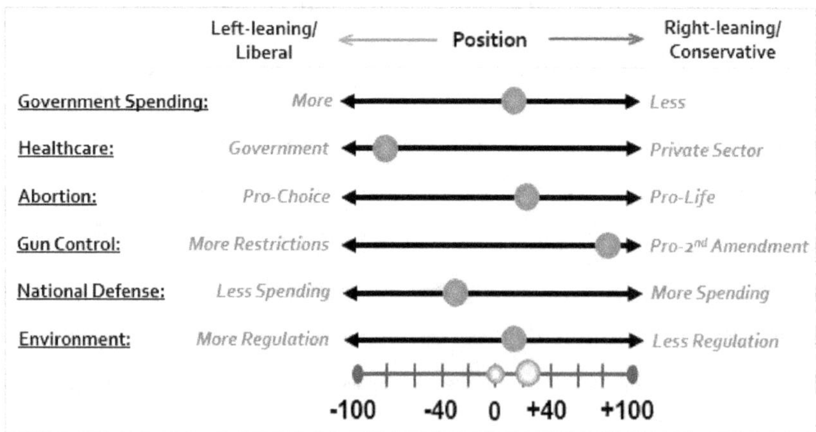

When, we calculate the data, a straight take on Martin's overall politics is that he is a near perfect centrist. The average of all his positions is 1.7—just about as close to 0 as you could get.

When we look at the weightings Martin assigns it balances a little more toward the right. Martin bases 50% of his political voting importance on gun control. Due to this out-sized issue of importance his overall score rolls right to 22.0. He may self-identify as conservative; or at least probably center-right.

Questions for analysis are whether Martin really is a moderate. Just because his average score is 1.7 does that really tell us as much as we would like. If all we were given was his average score without knowing anything about him, we might be surprised at his answers when we ask him about gun control. We would hear the passion he has on that issue.

If he called himself conservative but talks about how he is so thankful for the pre-existing coverage and his Obamacare plans, some on the right might question his politics.

Issue	Position	Ranking
Government Spending	10	5%
Healthcare	-90	25%
Abortion	20	10%
Gun Control	90	50%
National Defense	-30	10%
Environment	10	0%
SCORE	1.7	22.0

Charting political positions in a manner such as this (which includes the ranking of relative importance of issues compared to other issues) will help us gain more information about just what it is each of us really care about. If we only saw Martin's Nolan Chart score we wouldn't have any idea about the diversity of his positions on different issues.

An overall score does not really tell you much. Two voters could be 1.7 with completely opposite viewpoints. Moreover, Martin is not 1.7 overall because he is a chillaxed 1.7 on every issue. Contrarily, he holds some very strong views.

Thus, you start to notice differentiation among voters that might otherwise seem similar when you breakdown the analysis by stacking several issues together.

And you can see the 'volatility,' so to speak, in the range of their different opinions on a list of different issues.

Political pundits, the media and a lot of us as individuals just think all liberals or all conservatives are the same. We could get a lot further as a society if we recognized that there are people out there like Martin that are watching coverage about government healthcare benefits before they head out hunting.

These are relatively simplistic examples. Two takeaways.

First, this analysis could go so much deeper. On one hand, we can look at individuals for more and more issues. And, we can collect this information by surveying a pool of voters. Combining the findings to learn a lot more about groups we otherwise stereotype. There is a lot of research potential.

And the other takeaway is we need not take the analysis much further if we can grasp and internalize the simple findings that are right in front of us. That we only need to start talking a lot more with people we otherwise think we disagree with.

Connecting this to Candidates

We have different degrees of importance to different issues. Jane and Jack might both be very pro-life. However, they could still differ politically in that one believes it is a Federal issue and the other a States issue. Or, for example, Jane assesses the candidates and determines her vote solely on who she believes is most pro-life whereas Jack looks at the candidates with a broader filter and may be willing to sacrifice a little of his positions on pro-life in backing another candidate.

Do you know what their positions are? How do they align with you? If a candidate themselves is so far out in front of the rest of the candidates on a particular issue, and that is the most important issue to you—then it might not matter differences on other issues.

Conversely, the candidate could align with you on 9 out of 10 issues but what if the one you disagree on is your most important issue?

What is most important to a candidate--- or in a particular race—either does or does not line up with our views making certain candidates—or races—more or less critical in our mind.

These are all unpredictable factors. Which is why big changes can happen in debates. Also, not every voter hears the same news.

Overall, like individuals, candidates have a range of views. You could surely similarly score them. Another idea, for candidates as well as individuals could be plot views on a line in more of a 'bell curve'[30] kind of way. There are different ways of analysis—variation of a probability density function (say, broadly scattered or densely clustered). It helps just to visualize in your head merely to build understanding the diversity of each other's positions.

---

[30] For more on Bell Curves and standard deviation
http://robertniles.com/stats/stdev.shtml

14
SUB-QUESTIONS OF
POLITICAL ISSUES

Inside one topic are so many questions. Sub-questions of an issue. This is among our biggest problems in new conversations, forging new alliances and simply better understanding each other—any of us.

Are you "pro-choice" or "pro-life"?

Do you support protecting the environment?

These are broad, simple questions that don't even scratch the surface of the complexity of aspects within each issue.

**Every political topic has
dozens of sub-questions
And we might answer each sub-question
a little differently
So, an overall answer on a topic
Doesn't always tell us much at all**

First, the abortion issue. Being "pro-life" doesn't necessarily mean you want the federal government to ban all abortions. So, there is the position on the issue. And then there is the question of how would you want it addressed? It just gets too complex to sum up. Here are just some of the questions:

- Should the government provide taxpayer money for abortions?
- Should the federal government decide the issue of abortion?
- Should states instead be allowed to make their own legislation on abortion?
- Should late-term abortions be allowed?

- Should abortion after 20 weeks be allowed?
- Do you have a specific date that you define viability of a fetus?
- When do you believe life begins?
- If you are pro-life, is that for every situation? Are there exceptions? What exceptions do you support?
- Should healthcare workers be required to be a part of the abortion procedures even if they disagree with abortions for religious reasons?
- Should employers be required to provide abortion as part of their healthcare plans?
- Is a fetus a person? Does life begin at conception?
- Is it the right and choice of the woman whose body is involved; and whose financial future is inextricably impacted?
- Should government be involved at all?
- Should the "abortion pill" be outlawed?

The question of whether you are "pro-life" or "pro-choice" doesn't really mean all that much. With any issue, there are as many—or even lots more—questions.

**For each of several individual issues,
you will be to the right or to the left of
where you actually
classify yourself on the overall question.**

Next, on the environment issue. Sometimes it seems environmentalists hold that if someone doesn't believe in "global warming" that somehow that person is not reasonable on *any* aspect of the environmental cause.

There are a lot of questions within the environment topic in politics that are really all quite separate. For example, say, the Paris global climate accords. One can be opposed to what could properly be called a globalist-corporate agreement, while still being quite protective of the environment.

Let's consider a hypothetical voter, Dave.

Dave is a rural, conservative hunter. Dave sees no benefit to joining the Paris climate agreement and, also, Dave has all kinds of reasons he does not believe in "global warming." At the same time, environmentalists are doing themselves a total disservice by not recognizing that as a conservative hunter Dave is actually quite mindful about the earth. Dave wants to protect a lot of lands from over development. Dave is concerned long-term about ensuring fresh air and clean water. For Dave, it becomes a matter of talking about common sense approaches and solutions.

Here are several questions within the environment issue:

- Do you believe in global warming? Climate change?
- What do you believe is the cause of global warming?

- What is your level of concern about rising sea levels?
- Do you believe we need government-mandated caps on the amount of pollution?
- Do you support the private trading of 'carbon credit' on climate exchanges?
- Do you believe global accords are an important way to address environmental issues?
- Do you support fresh air?
- Do you support clean water?
- Do you believe the federal government has too many, or too few, environmental regulations?
- Do you support drilling in the Alaska National Wildlife Refuge? Do you support offshore drilling? If you live in one of the states where these issues directly affect you does your support change?
- Do you support the Keystone Pipeline? What about the Dakota Access portion of it?
- What is your level of concern about pollution in your local waters from any upstream manufacturing facilities that may be around?
- Protection of endangered species?
- Ethanol in gasoline?
- Do you support increasing fuel standards (such as miles per gallon targets) for vehicle production?
- Do you support tax credits for renewable energy? Do you support nuclear energy? Hydroelectricity? Coal? So-called 'fracking'? Wind turbines? Wind turbines if they are in your immediate area?
- Should we have more National Parks? More Federally-owned land protected for the environment?

What about national security and defense? It is perfectly rational for some people to want security. To some extent that may mean they are actually "all in" on growing the military with new weapons and "taking the fight to the enemy" or it could just mean they worry to some extent about wanting to preserve a life of pushing a stroller safely through their neighborhood or going for a jog and not worrying about terrorism or other invasions.

Whether their viewpoint is based on bad information or propaganda it is the view of an individual. Give people some space. Not everyone is a bad person for holding such and such a viewpoint. They don't necessarily hold that position for all of the reasons you oppose that position.

** People may not hold a position for
the same reasons you oppose that position. **

People don't always know the same information you know. They may not hear it and/or feel it the same way you do. You might be right! They might be totally wrong. But go into recognizing that they are entitled to see it a different way. Hard conversations with soft angles. Maybe, maybe *you* are wrong. At least that mindset can help. We cannot simply stereotype and judge everyone. And we shouldn't cut them off when we find out they are "pro-choice" or don't believe in global warming, or support a war. Until you delve a little deeper. What is their why? And how did they get those opinions?

Understanding Survey Questions:

Let's take the issue of defense—national security.

A survey question: Do you support more national defense spending?

My 'yes' or 'no' answer to that question is 'no' (we will get deeper into that answer in a second… first, continuing).

Then the survey follows up on that question by asking, well 'how important (on a scale of 0-to10) is that issue?' And, right there I am lost. What do they mean? Are they asking as a matter of that issue versus other issues? So how important is national security to me? Which takes me back to the first question. Because the wording is asking if I support *more… spending*. Or, are they asking how important (or intense) is my answer? Which was 'no'? Like, are they asking how much I want to cut defense spending?

So, if I answer '0' out of 10 will that make me "totally against national defense spending" or "0" as in this issue isn't really that important to me.

How is their algorithm written? How do they *take* my answer?

I think all of us feel this way a lot of times taking political surveys.

Kind of throw our hands up.

There are going to be all kinds of different perspectives that make this (or any) issue hard to boil down to simple answers. Others could view national security as their life-or-death issue and be terrified of the risks from terrorism and other countries. That same person could be more concerned than me about overall government spending and yet answer wanting way more spending on national defense. Go figure!

Now consider a survey question asking how pro-choice or pro-life are you on a scale of 0 to 10. You sit there and wonder how to answer the question. You are kind of in the middle. In other words, what flashes through your head is sub-questions such as those above. And you think that for some of those sub-topics you are pro-choice and for others you are pro-life.

When we put multiple top-line topics together for analysis we found people can have a very strongly held conservative opinion and at the same time a strongly held liberal viewpoint on a different topic. That goes for sub-questions in a topic too. So, answering 5 as being halfway between pro-life and pro-choice does not necessarily mean you are ho-hum about sub-questions. You might be very, very passionate that women must have the right to choose and at the same time be equally passionate that after 20 weeks no way, no how. But, if a survey asks you 0 to 10 and you must put something.

That is where surveys don't necessarily tell the full story.

This could go on-and-on for different topics. For example, national defense and foreign policy could have all kinds of sub-questions. The federal budget. Sub-questions could be about overall spending levels, the deficit, every line item within the budget, and so on.

Each voter than has their individual answers to these questions.

Some voters care about abortion and have a definitive answer for every sub-question on that topic. Whereas others care more about a different issue.

You might not have an answer for a lot of questions.

Or you might have an opinion but defer to others that you are comfortable know more, and/or are looking into it more than you ever could or care to.

Do you care about every little sub-question?
Do you feel you know enough to answer?
Are you fine with other people deciding certain of these?
Which ones matter more-or-less to you?

It is all a lot more complex than our media likes to make us think.

Do you average out your opinions?

Do you support a stronger military? Two people both answer 'yes.' But what does that mean? Each person could have completely different ideas about what their preference is.

You can make a judgment call, as we did above, to place yourself somewhere along the line above. However, the fact of the matter is that the answer you give is based sometimes on averaging out your actual positions. And *that* becomes your placement on a line or in a chart result. For each of several individual issues, you will be to the right or to the left of where you classified yourself. You too have a bell curve of political viewpoints.

It is hard to form any stereotypes if we delve into issues a little deeper.

We can and may change our viewpoints. Others may change us. What is your likelihood of changing your position on an issue? And for candidates? Why do they change positions? Sometimes it *is* the lobbyist influence and donor contributions. Other times perhaps they are making the best decision for the people they represent. And, still more, the legislation at hand is usually a sub-question. Aspects of legislation usually deal in sub-questions.

15
WHO IS A MODERATE?
IS IT WHAT IT SEEMS?

Who is a Centrist/Moderate?

When you consider the vast range of issues for everyone; calling someone "liberal" or "conservative" is too narrow a definition. Same with the center, and moderates.

It is far too simplistic to call someone a centrist and/or to call yourself a moderate.

As we have seen in our analysis, summing up your views into a formula and finding you average out on all issues doesn't really make you a centrist.

You *are* a centrist (moderate) on the *individual issues* you are a centrist (moderate) on. So, on one issue at a time we can clearly find who is moderate on that specific issue.

There are two other ways I think people can be centrist/moderate.

First, can you understand where other people are coming from? Are you willing to listen?

Second, do you like to negotiate and compromise? Can you work deals?

<u>Moderates?</u>
An individual issue clearly has moderates
With many issues, eventually there are ones you are not moderate on
That said,
One: can you listen to all other perspectives? And understand.
Two: can you compromise and negotiate with anyone.

The interesting thing about the two points above is that it doesn't matter—at all—what your positions are. You could be the most liberal person in the world. Every one of your viewpoints could be the most liberal out there, and yet if you possess traits like this I believe that is a real key to leading new politics.

Can you genuinely be interested in viewpoints that could be from out of left field and/or completely different than what you were thinking and/or what you agree with?

Do you like finding new solutions? A so-called "third way" that can get some of what you want while also helping others to get what they want? Can you facilitate dialogue among others? Helping others to find common ground.

If you believe you are a moderate, you probably are. In the sense that you likely know in your heart and mind that you do approach others and individual issues in these manners. Because of this…

The other interesting thing is that a lot more people are moderate then we are lead to believe.

A lot more people are "moderate" than we are lead to believe

In other words, just because you are "too far right" or "too far left" or a little more off center on many issues than society says is moderate is not looking at it right.

Society, the media, the political establishment has their own ideas and definitions for what a centrist and moderate are. It is self-serving.

You could be way out there on an extreme. However, if you possess that sincerity to talk with anyone. If you *want* to find compromises. You could still facilitate agreements on tough issues.

On the second point, you may want to call yourself a centrist or moderate because you are left of center on one issue and right of center on another issue. While the person standing next to you also calls themselves a centrist while holding the exact opposite view on both issues. Neither of you would agree! Unless, you compromise. That is an essence in defining what a centrist or moderate is. Can you compromise on those positions? And/or can you help others to find ways to compromise on issues?

We could go issue-by-issue and you can find the centrists and moderates based by their answers on the issue in question. But is that even the right way to find the best solution. What if the opposite sides of an issue could hash out an agreement?

Give yourself more credit.

Or give the right people credit.

For our future, the people that should be more involved in politics are those that can put people first. We need more politicians that are in it for the people. That is the type of compromise and moderate we need.

16
WHERE IS THE CENTER?

Where is the center? Consider the United States of America. Do we measure the center based on population? Based on geography?

Do we measure the center of the country by geography? So, Kansas. Do we include Alaska? Alaska is about the size of 10 Midwest states combined. Including Alaska moves the center up a bit and over to the west—just about into Montana.

Or do we determine the center based on population? As of 2010, that would be southern Missouri.[31] And that is the *mean* center. There is also a *median* population center. In Indiana![32]

So, it can get complicated even with rather simple questions.

What makes the political center, the center?

When we consider the House of Representatives, we measure the center by the leaders of two political parties getting together?

This has really no bearing on our geographic representation. And the viewpoints of these leaders may only relate to a small percentage of Americans views.

Who is a centrist?

What makes a centrist?

---

[31] https://www.census.gov/dataviz/visualizations/050/

[32] Median population center: https://www2.census.gov/geo/pdfs/reference/cenpop2010/centerpop_median2010.pdf More reading: https://www.census.gov/geo/reference/centersofpop.html

Why is the center of the House of Representatives measured by the leaders of two political parties?

"Centrists" (such as the "Gang of Five" and such) currently get a lot of credit in society for being able to mix a little of the left and a little of the right to move us forward.

But our current definition kind of defines what that center is.

And it limits our true potentials.

For new ideas. And for more innovative solutions.

The Traditional Political Spectrum

⟵———————————————⟶

Far Left   Center   Far Right
Liberal   Moderate   Conservative

The current political establishment has kind of branded themselves as a "centrist" of a certain mentality. That they are above the fray. They can reach agreements with others that are with the opposite party.

Extremists? Or a part of Better Solutions?

A bigger issue with the vertical line and its end points is that if the center is a moderate we end up viewing those that are further and further from the center as being bigger and bigger problems.

The farther away from center you are, the more extremist you are labeled by society. That isn't helpful. It is not fair to a "far-right" conservative. And it isn't fair to judge "radical" liberals that way either.

We all have unique perspectives and the problem with the left-right narrative is that certain ideas are viewed as too extreme to be acceptable. We can't even dialogue about it.

Are extreme elements of the parties a problem? Part of the mystique behind the campaigns of Donald Trump and Bernie Sanders was their ability on the campaign trail to tap into these extremes for messages that connected with voters. Voters want diversity of thinking. And new ideas. Fresh approaches. Different. They are tired of same old, same old. And they seem to like populist messages. Thus, likely they would like populist governing and populist laws.

The current mindset around the political spectrum is divisive in nature. It precludes a lot of conversation. How could anyone possibly leapfrog that far to even talk with anyone across the political spectrum? ...In order to form political alliances beyond party and to see where possible agreements lie is to look beyond a simple spectrum of left to right. There should not be just one center.

Party Politics: Democrats and Republicans

Leaders of the Democrat and Republican Party often end up being closer to the other party then the middle of their own party. In this diagram is a hypothetical example showing ideologically where the leader of the Democratic Party and Republican Party are based a) on the traditional left-right spectrum but also b) within the ideological span of their party.

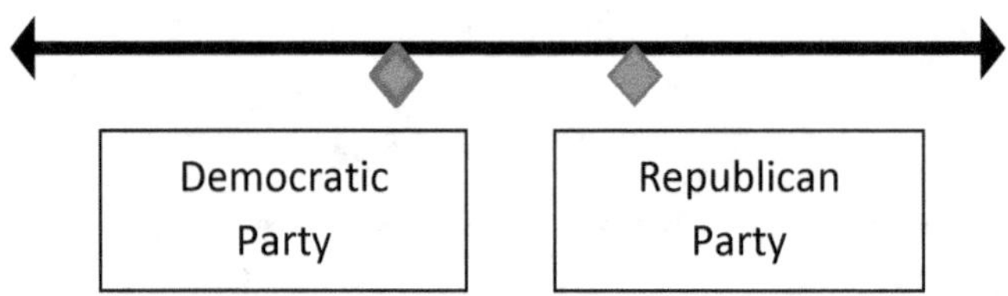

Now, in reality, the truth gets even messier. The ideological span of each party overlaps (there are Democrats that are right or center and Republicans that are left of center. There are Democrats that are ideologically left of center. And there are Republicans that are ideologically right of center.

Control of the 2 major parties is not even at the center of the 2 political parties.

How do you define the 'center' of a political party? Who is in control of the political party? And what are their positions on the issues?

The center of the Democratic Party should not be the people closest to the Republicans. And similarly, the center of the Republican Party should not be the representatives that are closest to the Democrats. That is a chosen alignment. There can be other alignments.

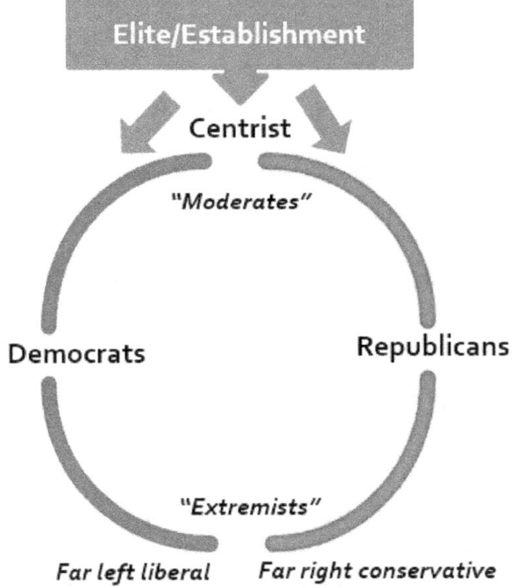

Two arrows overlaying the matrix below help to illustrate that we are missing how to define alignments. The leadership of the Republican and Democratic parties is not in the center of those parties. Control of the parties is closer to the center.

Control of the Political Parties

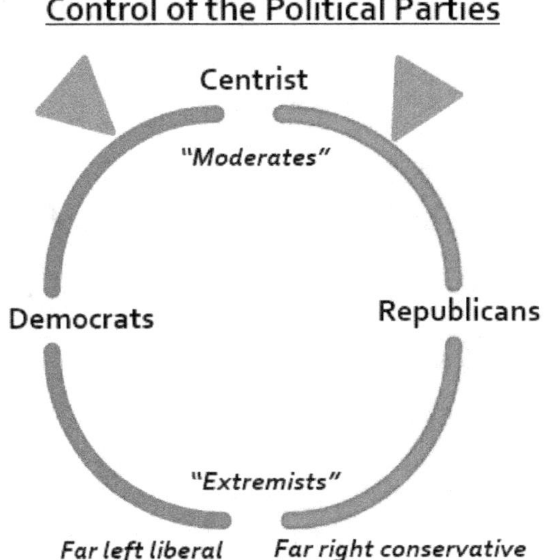

Why are centrists, centrists? They compromise. People at the extreme of one end of the spectrum or the other are not seeing the broader potential in their views and positions because on the political spectrum they look out from one end or the other and try to get acknowledged.

The centrists are willing to give up some of their beliefs. Or, perhaps more succinctly, they sacrifice the beliefs of those they represent (those that voted for them). The current center is the center because they agree to work together. Currently, society sees this as the only way of possibility for agreement is in the middle of this static line.

It is virtually impossible for millions of people to tie themselves to one of 2 parties all the way down. Even on major issues there can be differences? Candidates of the same party hardly agree on most, let alone all issues. So, the myriad of possibilities of the extent of agreement is infinite.

How much of your party are you?

Even the most steadfast of Democrats is not likely to be in 100% agreement with 100% of the platform of the Democratic Party. Using the cone cylinder concept introduced earlier, the diagram helps to visualize how much of the population is truly deeply aligned to one party or the other. Most people, more-or-less will pick one side or the other, however, it becomes fewer and fewer people that are dedicated on issue-after-issue to one of the major parties. And at the most extreme it is a true 'unicorn' to find the handful of people that are 100% aligned. There are party loyalists to be sure. Mostly, it involves the ones with a vested power and financial benefit from the party—the deepest establishment elements of the party. And they are outliers in society. Protecting the party more than they are concerned about the interest of the people.

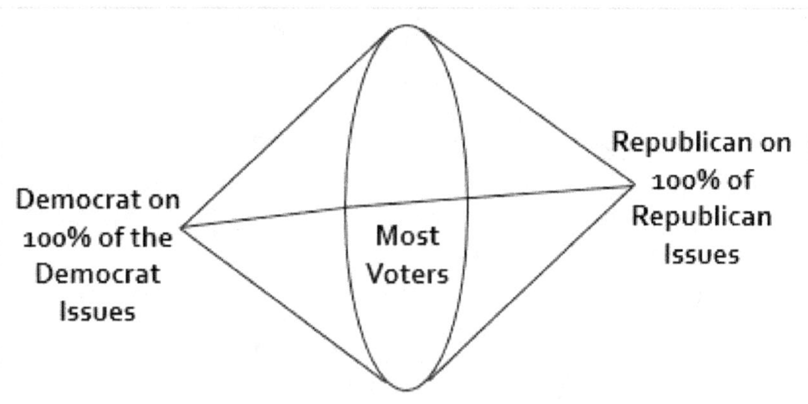

There is a difference between "most likely to vote Democrat" and those that "agree the most with the entire Democratic Party platform." In other words, the voter that is most likely to vote Democrat may not agree with all parts of the Democratic Party platform. It is just that they may be more liberal on certain key issues that are most important to them and they can't imagine the alternative of not voting for the Democratic Party.

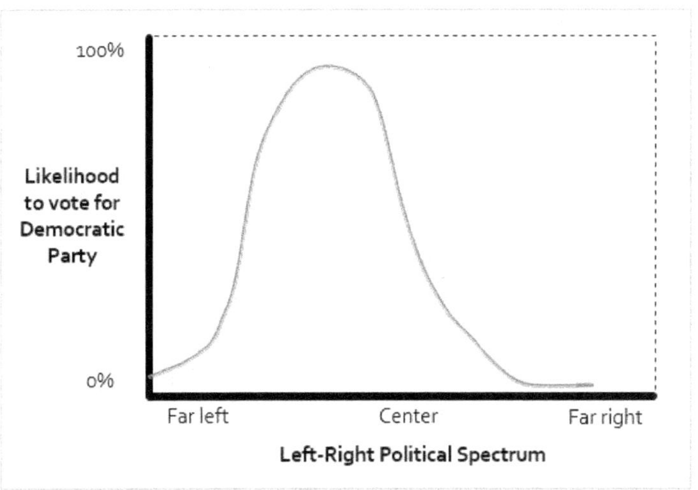

The 'best' Democrat is not the furthest left Democrat. The most reliable Democrat voter will be the party establishment and those closest to the center of Democrat positions. Centrist-leaning Democrats will occasionally vote Republican. And far-left leaning Democrats may stay home or vote for a third party alternative.

Every party could be said to have its establishment. Its founders, funders, those with close ties. These people have stakes in the game and go in whatever direction. Some less motivated by and of the interest in the party—in fact perhaps totally opposed to some—but they get perks of power.

So, do we only have 1 political party?

Many of the Republicans around the 'red dot' (in the diagram) and many of the Democrats around the 'blue dot' are happy to switch parties if it means staying in power.

The center of power is really the points between the red dot and the blue dot.

The reality of this centrist compromise is that the real core principle for agreement is perpetuating their own power and that of the current economic structure.

BEYOND
REPUBLICANS AND DEMOCRATS

Does the U.S. have only 1 political party? Can we move beyond this? Two slightly different versions of the same thing. Led by powerful corporate and big banker interests no matter which party you vote for.

Borrowing the type of diagram I used in the "Quantum Politics" chapter here we can place "establishment politicians" at the end of the cylinder. A small group of people. Yet, with an outsized political clout.

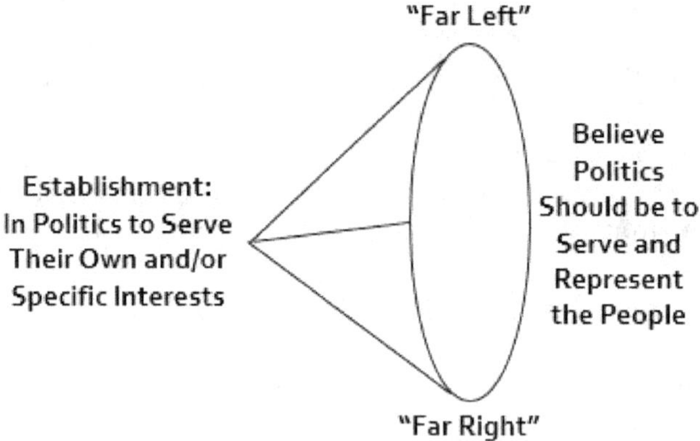

Changes the narrative. Who are the outliers? Whatever you want to call everyone that is not part of the establishment the point here is that it is a small sliver of people that are a part of the "political establishment"—the so-called "centrists," and self-declared "gangs." They are a "Gang of Five," yes, a handful of people out there as their own form of outlier.

There is little difference between the power centers of the two parties so much as who is behind the scenes controlling that ultimately each party is running within toleration bands for the most aggressive of big money establishment elements.

Money

The current two-party system *does* revolve around **money**. However, the commonly held conception is that one party, the Republicans are the big money party. This is economically not the case.

If you have a dollar to spend to influence legislation where will you spend it? You will spend it where you have the opportunity to get your legislation passed.[33]

Big corporations and the large Wall Street banks and power brokers do not pick one side or the other. That would far too risky. As professor Carroll Quigley noted in his infamous political treatise Tragedy and Hope, with two virtually identical parties "the American people can 'throw the rascals out' at any election without leading to any profound or extreme shifts in policy."[34]

Elections are in most cases planned out long, long before their time by the establishment. This part is not a conspiracy, nor a fault. It is a fact. It is prudent, it is wise, and it is the way it is. Establishment elements do not want to risk things to chance. Candidates are laid out well in advance. The pieces are put in place. Plans are made.

The establishment elements do not merely reside in the Republican Party and leave their business success in the hands of the people and a potential loss of power should their Party lose. The large banks. The big corporations. They are behind both sides. One way or the other they are going to rest assured they will have politicians friendly to their cause. It is far too narrow minded for any to believe money is one party or the other.

Beating the Establishment

Going back to the French Revolution, and our discussion of the origins of the right and the left.

Today, loyalists to the King would be in the center. Today's center perpetuates Washington, DC power. Today's center perpetuates corporate, banker dominance.

That doesn't make everything a centrist does as 'bad' or always corporate/banker friendly. But the point needs to be understood. As it can

---

[33] This hints at another possible benefit of a two-party system. If one party has too much money chasing, then the price of buying their influence goes up and the alternative option becomes cheaper. That there is almost a level of parity that exists in a two-party system.

[34] http://www.ourrepubliconline.com/Author/60

help those on the fringe 'extremes' to see how, or why, they might have cause for agreement.

It was, for lack of a better word, "economic centrists" that were at the far right in the original meaning. The original right in France had allegiance to concentration of power in decision-making. Today, it is centrists forming "gangs of 8" that are the center of economic and political power.

There has been the "Gang of Eight"[35] and the "Gang of Five"[36] and such to lump together the "centrist" mix of Democrats and Republicans that get together to move otherwise bottlenecked legislation forward. The point is that, for the sake of power, there are certain aspects people leave at the table. Odd, to use the term "gang" but alas.

David A. Stockman in *The Great Deformation*—his treatise on corruption in capitalism—believes the real divide in America is with the establishment versus the people. The left-right battle is not America's biggest problem.

Stockman: "The biggest political divide in America in years to come will not be between the Republican and Democratic parties. It will be between (the powerful banks and corporations) that has fixed the economic and political game to their liking, and the vast majority who, as a result, find themselves in a fix."[37]

How to fix this? In the words of Thomas Jefferson, "the two enemies of the people are criminals and government, so let us tie the second down with the chains of the constitution so the second will not become the legalized version of the first."[38]

The power of the establishment. And the manner in which the powers of the Democratic Party work with the powers of the Republican Party are why many people are losing faith in having a voice in Washington, DC. Many don't even vote anymore. What is the difference?

Bipartisan: The New Dirty Word

"Bipartisan" should be reclassified as a dirty word. I know the types in Washington, DC that use the term "bipartisan." They are the establishment. They are the corporate bought politicians. They are the Wall Street politicians.

Hacks that claim to be "bipartisan" like to use the term because it is taken as kind of a shield. "Bipartisan" is taken at face value as synonymous with 'above the fray' and above the politics of the 'extreme' right and left.

---

[35] https://en.wikipedia.org/wiki/Gang_of_Eight_(immigration)

[36] https://www.thedenverchannel.com/news/politics/gang-of-five-bipartisan-group-of-senators-working-to-extend-daca-before-years-end

[37] *The Great Deformation,* David A. Stockman. 2013.

[38] https://www.monticello.org/site/jefferson/two-enemies-people-are-criminals-and-governmentquotation

Working with others is absolutely the right approach. So, the point is not that compromise is somehow bad.

The point is: what are you compromising *for?*

To me, one of the greatest lines in politics was Denis Kucinich questioning Goldman Sachs banker, Neel Kashkari: "I don't think anyone questions, Mr. Kashkari, that you're working hard. Our question is, who you're working for?"[39] Kashkari, stepped away from the bank to run the government's TARP program—right amid the 2008 financial crisis—giving away taxpayer money to the biggest banks.[40][41]

The instinct is to believe that politicians trying to work a deal between Democrats and Republicans is the right approach. And, anyone working a deal—absolutely—I support working together!

However, "bipartisan" has become a combination of the worst elements of both parties. Compromising in *this* middle is not a compromise that benefits the people. Rather it is a self-serving path taken by corporate-funded, Washington DC establishment politicians. The "bipartisan" politicians are actually the most self-serving, highest-funded and longest-tenured in Washington, DC. They do not represent the people.

And, the elements in control want to keep this power. They plan it out. Goldman Sachs is one step ahead of the American people.

When you put the nightly news broadcast on your TV. When you turn on "Face the Nation" or "Meet the Press" you are getting the hand-chosen corporate politicians towing the line. The message the establishment wants you to hear. You are not getting diversity of ideas. And you get fed drama. Imaginary fighting between the two parties. And the result is 'solutions' that sound so right.

Goldman Sachs has gotten good at running 'made for Hollywood' campaigns. Barack Obama was legendary. Greek columns at a massive outdoor rally in Denver. Donald Trump too. Massive rallies. A real movement in both cases. Hope and Change. Make America Great Again. Both, very populist in their tone and messaging. And yet, Obama in office was obviously an 8-year loss for anyone that may have thought he would help them. What did we get instead? The biggest stock market rally in history. Trump? Lots of talk; but then who comes in to run the Trump White House? Goldman Sachs. Everywhere.[42]

---

[39] https://www.youtube.com/watch?v=VrLDje8itdg

[40] http://www.motherjones.com/politics/2008/11/dennis-kucinich-investigates-treasurys-blank-check/

[41] Note, Neel Kashkari's reward for his efforts on behalf of the bankers during the 2008 crisis—Kashkari is now candidate for U.S. Senate in California.

[42] https://theintercept.com/2017/09/17/goldman-sachs-gary-cohn-donald-trump-administration/ and

It's not the government we need. It is not by the people. It is not for the people. How to beat this?

The future is outside these establishment elements and getting some new political parties and new political movements.

---

https://www.commondreams.org/views/2017/10/15/government-sachs-and-trump-administration and
http://thehill.com/homenews/administration/324027-trump-names-another-goldman-sachs-exec-to-senior-administration-role.

18
YELLOW STATES

Not blue or red. Yellow States.

Why yellow? A little background first.

Red and blue states will soon give way. Not to purple. To yellow states.

Purple states are a combination of red and blue. That is not the future. A purple state is nicely balanced to suit the establishment. But it is not radically different. And it is not the path of an innovative America.

Yellow takes us to a brighter future. Why yellow?

Today, the political map is divided up into traditional "red states" and "blue states." States that are primarily held by the Democrats (Democratic Party) have come to be called "blue states". States in which the Republicans (GOP) win are the "red states".

Blue State	Red State
Democratic Party	Republican Party

In the 1996 Presidential election, Ross Perot followed up his 1992 independent candidacy with a third party run as part of the Reform Party. In 1996, Perot's luster waned a bit (from the 18.9% of the popular vote he received nationally); receiving 8.4% of the vote. However, just like 1992, Ross Perot did not win any states and therefore had 0 electoral college votes. The electoral college votes were split among the winner, Bill Clinton, of the Democratic Party and his challenger from the Republican Party Bob Dole. The results: Clinton won 31 states to Bob Dole 19 states. These results are shown in the map below as red states (Dole, GOP) and blue states (Clinton,

Democrats).

Map from Wikipedia[43]

If both the Democrats and the Republicans are represented in the state rather equally we often use purple. "Purple States" are those that have a fairly equal mix of Democrats and Republicans. Or in the case of analyzing one election, purple may reflect a state too close to call.

Purple State
Part Republican, Part Democrat

Purple is a good mix of saying a little bit of Republican and a little bit of Democrat. For example, each state has 2 U.S. Senators. A purple state would have 1 Republican and 1 Democrat in the U.S. Senate. In other words, purple states are essentially those that are ½ red state and ½ blue state.

The composition of the U.S. Senate in early 2018 included 12 "purple states" represented by 1 Republican and 1 Democrat.[44]

But… what purple does not mean is independent.

Purple doesn't mean a third party. Or something different.

Purple states could be said to have voters with more independence in that they don't always vote for the same party.

---

[43] Map on Wikipedia
https://en.wikipedia.org/wiki/File:ElectoralCollege1996.svg via
https://en.wikipedia.org/wiki/United_States_presidential_election,_1996
[44] Nevada, Montana, North Dakota, Colorado, Missouri, Alabama, Florida, Indiana, Ohio, West Virginia and Pennsylvania per
https://en.wikipedia.org/wiki/115th_United_States_Congress#Senate_3

However, the point here is to identify a color that can represent breaking completely free of voting for a Democrat or a Republican.

So…

How do we categorize what happens if neither Democrats or Republicans win? Well, in some cases the answer might obviously come to us. For example, if the Green Party of the United States (GPUS) made traction and won, for example, a couple Senate seats in a state than we could naturally call that a "Green State."

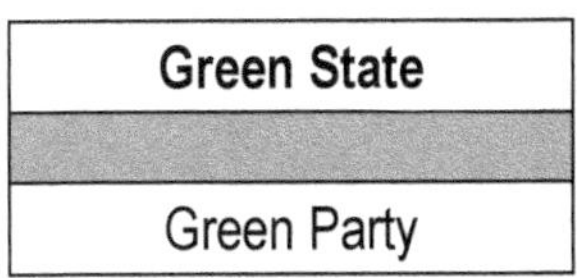

But, what about cases which may not be so easy? What do we call those states? And where are these colors coming from anyway? Using Red States and Blue States is certainly natural considering the U.S. flag.

Flag of the United States of America[45]

So, if there is something other than a Democrat or Republican maybe it should be a "White State"? Red, white, and blue. For obvious reasons, we don't want to label any state "white." Or, black. We don't want to have "white states" or "black states." Unless, let's say things got a little crazy and the "New Black Panther" party[46] won a couple Senate seats in a state.

Regarding the use of red and blue. Beyond the connection to our flag: blue and red are both primary colors.

The other primary color? Of which there are three.

Yellow.

In picking a color for independents, the answer for us can stand out plain

---

[45] https://en.wikipedia.org/wiki/Flag_of_the_United_States#/media/File:Flag_of_the_United_States.svg

[46] See http://cbpm.org/nbpp.html, http://www.nbpp.org/home.html or http://www.latimes.com/nation/la-na-new-black-panthers-20160714-snap-story.html.

as day in the color wheel diagram below.

An independent state can be marked as yellow. Yellow is the other primary color that is opposed to Blue and Red. The primary color wheel, as shown below, emphasizes Blue, Red and Yellow that are each 4 separated by three colors in between them.

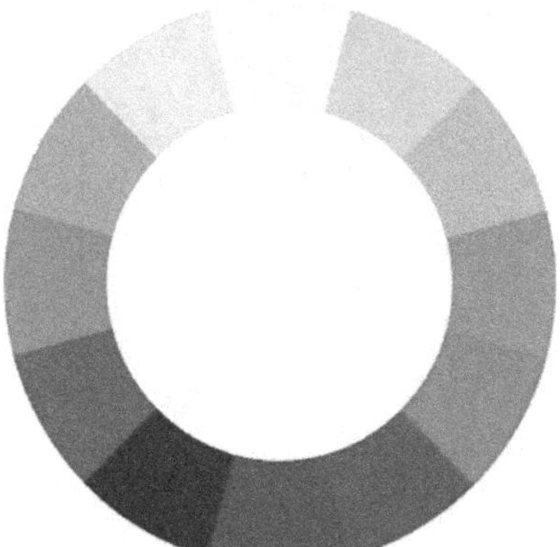

RYB/BYR Color Wheel[47]

There are different ways to classify colors, known as "color models." For example, RGB and CMYK primary colors.[48]

RYB (Red, Yellow, Blue) is the historical origin of the color wheel and the basis for mixing colors for art and design, such as painting.

All of this evolved out of the work that began with legendary physicist Isaac Newton. Isaac Newton approached colors as a physicist trying to understand light and his research would take him into directions that would discover and develop classical mechanics, such as gravity. Newton, and a rival member of the Royal Society, Robert Hooke, were working to understand light. They believed light must either be a wave or particles.[49] Newton used prisms to show that light alone was responsible for color. By 1672 he had refracted white light with a prism and showed all the component colors of a rainbow.[50] Eventually, Newton published a "visible spectrum"[51] regarding

---

[47] https://en.wikipedia.org/wiki/Primary_color#/media/File:BYR_color_wheel.svg

[48] For more information about the Primary Colors and the color model groupings RGB, CMYK and RYB visit
https://en.wikipedia.org/wiki/Primary_color

[49] http://www.thestargarden.co.uk/Newtons-theory-of-light.html

[50] http://www.webexhibits.org/colorart/bh.html

[51] By 1704 Newton described the relationship between colors as a spectrum. This so-called "Visible Spectrum" was published as part of his seminal publication on colors, *Opticks: or, a treatise of the reflexions, refractions,*

reflection and refraction of light.[52] To make a long story short, there is a scientific basis to this color wheel and how the primary colors complement each other.[53]

Below is Newton's original visible spectrum oriented from the left side as red all the way around to violet.[54]

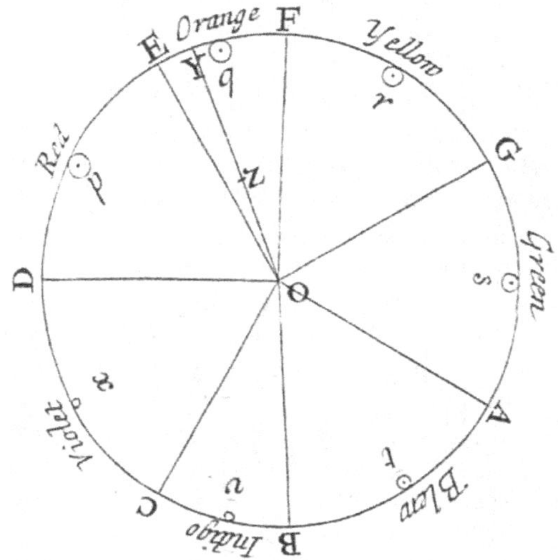

Isaac Newton *Visible Spectrum*[55]

Thus, as early as the late 1600's Isaac Newton began to unravel and describe the relationship of colors in new and totally different ways. Prior to Newton light was viewed as various combinations of light and darkness.

David Brewster's 1831 three primary explanation of spectral hues as overlapping red, yellow and blue light. And that work led to even deeper research by A. Thomas Young and B. Helmholtz in which an orangish-red,

---

inflexions and colours of light (Newton, Isaac, 1704, first edition) https://en.wikipedia.org/wiki/Opticks

[52] https://en.wikipedia.org/wiki/Visible_spectrum and http://www.thestargarden.co.uk/Newtons-theory-of-light.html.

[53] Newton discovered the refracting of light as colors ranging from red (the least refrangible) to a deep violet (the most refrangible).

[54] Some call this model "ROY G BIV" for Red-Orange-Yellow, Green and Blue-Indigo-Violet, the seven colors of a rainbow. http://munsell.com/color-blog/sir-isaac-newton-color-wheel/

[55] As published in *Opticks* in 1704 https://en.wikipedia.org/wiki/Visible_spectrum#/media/File:Newton%27s_color_circle.png

solid green and a violet-leaning blue where the three primary colors.[56]

Today, there is a wide variety of bold interpretations to understanding colors. You can look at myriads of different interpretations[57] and read all about it.[58] Primary, secondary and tertiary color analysis;[59] Hues, tint, tone and shade.[60]

There can be incredible differential nuance created in images from colors that are so close together on the color wheel.[61] You can make a full picture out of basically the same colors—the "hue" of the color is all that changes.[62][63] "A color scheme that lives inside a narrow range of hues is said to be analogous."[64]

And so, it is with our individual politics. A lot more nuance and variety—even among those that seem to be nearly the same.

We need new variety in our politics.

Yellow states. Not red states. Not blue states. Not purple. We need innovation. To retain the greatness of America, its people need to blast into the future.

New political alignments. A new third party filled with a truly independent, positive energy are possible.

People are tired of the same old politics. And, I believe the people will soon tire of the same old political establishment. That is *why* we should see yellow state politics emerge.

So… *how* will these yellow states come about? What new political alignments are possible. And… *when* will this occur.

---

[56] http://www.huevaluechroma.com/062.php

[57] https://www.pinterest.com/pin/241857442465319007/

[58] For a detailed summary of many aspects of color theory, read more at: https://medium.muz.li/the-ultimate-ux-guide-to-color-design-4d0a18a706ed

[59] https://color-wheel-artist.com/primary-colors/

[60] https://color-wheel-artist.com/hue/

[61] https://medium.com/retronator-magazine/down-the-color-wheel-with-merrigo-226ad1be0623

[62] https://cdn-images-1.medium.com/max/600/1*HUl40SHfO3kP0OaRMTE0KQ.png

[63] https://cdn-images-1.medium.com/max/600/1*5EHS1M6LrUjr8Jr2iJrCzA.png

[64] https://medium.com/retronator-magazine/down-the-color-wheel-with-merrigo-226ad1be0623

19

NEW POLITICAL ALIGNMENTS

Likely to be totally new people. Likely outside the political mainstream. Not likely to be covered by the media. Probably not going to get very positive media coverage.

Shacking up a powerful cabal of old, stale, entrenched political power is not going to be easy. Ironically, they are the ones getting the glamorous media coverage. They will also work swiftly to co-op any competitive movements. And, believe me, they are planning ahead and plotting any range of ways to ensure retaining power. They are recruiting their new talent and planning the Hollywood-style campaigns that generate excitement throughout the population.

So, the challenge for new political alignments is to rise above all that noise and breakthrough all the hurdles in the way. The establishment has spent decades passing the legislation that locks them deeper into power. It is so hard just to get on the ballot.[65] And so any new political parties and alternative candidates need to navigate those challenges. And good luck getting the word out. That will take real effort.

Structural changes to political power are also more than likely. For example, how we vote. How we decide who wins. And, how we are represented in the legislative branch. I call it "Democracy 2.0." I believe there will be more direct voting (such as referendums; and, so-called "participatory democracy"[66]) as well. The main point however is concepts such as "proportional representation"—in which, if 5% of the people vote for a very

---

[65] And as another example, the Presidential debates and how it is hard for any third party candidates to get included.

[66] *The Future and its Enemies*, 1998, Virginia Postrel, Pp 21.

liberal or very conservative party they will receive 5% of the seats in Congress. This will enable a lot bolder leadership and innovative new ideas as politicians will be free to really express the depth of their understanding and ingenuity. Because voters will be able to 'stay true' to their own views and vote for the politicians they *want* to vote for. Not the ones they are stuck voting for the so-called 'lesser of two evils.'

All of this is on the way.

New political alignments—forged out of this coming era of bi-politics;[67] and syncretic politics,[68] such as this book.

The center of politics does not need to be what we have been told. Practically, one might say the center is the middle of what gets enough votes to pass. In the House of Representatives, with **435 members**, it takes 217 votes to pass a bill. In other words, if a bill is passed by 217 Democrats the only relevant point is that it passed and became law. More than half the representatives voted for it. Something that passes may not be considered "mainstream" but it has received a plurality of votes.

Those 217 votes could come from anywhere. It shouldn't matter where you can get 217 votes so long as you can stitch together the support of 217. *That* becomes your center. Or that becomes the goal for successful politics. In this sense "Democracy 2.0" also needs to work at shattering the party-based power structure of our House and Senate. All legislation needs to channel through party leadership. That is something that could be changed to something more positive.

There are so many elements to new alignments. It is not a matter of aligning on all issues. It is a matter of determining what are the core issues to form alliance around.

One thing is very likely…

New political alignments will only be possible out of different combinations of people talking together and working out new paths forward. Thus, a change in political dialogue is necessary.

Key criteria for positive change include:

- Appreciation of independent views
- Appreciation of other people's views
- Critical thinking. Important for society. Need to teach it.
- Alternative solutions forged through intense dialogue with those

---

[67] Bi-politics is expressed in this book as those that hold views aligning with both the Republican Party and the Democratic Party without necessarily meaning they are a moderate, or centrist, in the conventional thinking. Moreover, their votes may swing from one party to the next.

[68] Syncretic politics view political perspectives outside the conventional left-right spectrum.

you don't agree with.

The future is likely to reward those that boldly band together against conventional wisdom as well as, more importantly, those that start reaching out for dialogue with the intent of action with people you might not agree with.

None of this is to say leave your own principles at the door. The point is to see which principles you can work around.

Compromise is the overriding element of successful politics. We are all different. An important premise behind this book is opening eyes and minds and indirectly guide people to a new era of compromise in politics. New leaders do not need to compromise your positions or values; but only learn to work with a new set of people and explore completely new ideas. Voters around the country are ready to break our stagnation.

20
FUTURE
POLITICAL PARTIES

The major political parties certainly change and evolve. A Republican today is not the same as 100 years ago. Same with Democrats. Over time, the positions of each party have wavered and changed.

To some extent it goes beyond party. It is about the individual candidate. It should always be about the candidate.

The future of political parties could be with much less alignment based on core issues. For example, candidate transparency could be the defining aspect of a party. In other words, the candidates for a new political party could be selected based, primarily, on their willingness answer an in-depth political survey. Transparency to voters. The party brings to the voters candidates that you know where they stand. Simple. So long as you truthfully, honestly and openly answer the **<u>survey questions</u>**, you are a party member. People can decide if they want to vote for you based on reviewing your answers—as well as all the typical aspects of their ongoing campaign.

In this way, there could be no party at all. And independents themselves could make themselves better known and understood by the voters by submitting to this type of transparency. Candidates run on who they are and where they stand. Independents.

Voters will know more about
where a candidate stands by
what *that candidate's* positions are
than those of any party they might belong to.

This helps with accountability in office too. Today, an establishment politician can sell out the base of their party on a core issue, but we never knew where they stood in the first place. Transparency can help make for accountable politicians. *And...* help voters make informed selections.

The future of political parties could even get deeper than that...

Political parties could be based entirely on **mindsets**. Do you have the right *mindset* to be a part of this party? A political party that works to solve problems. Commits itself to finding innovative new solutions. Filled with politicians and members that commit to dialogue. Commit to respecting each other.

In other words, finding the right ideas.

Without subscribing to any notion that Mike Huckabee represents the future, or a real alternative, he has, at least, tapped into—and expresses—this least this way of thinking. He calls it **"vertical politics."**[69] Not right. Not left. But what is good for everyone vs. what is bad for everyone. Instead of is the policy left or right. Is it going to help? Does it take us up? Or does it drag us down? Looking at issues and possible solutions vertically.[70] An aspirational perspective of a twist on this horizontal line.

Future political parties could also define themselves more by their **process and rules**. How is their leadership determined? How open is this process? For example, the followers of this type of party might be inspired by the fact that there is a transparent, non-bureaucratic organizational structure that de-emphasizes the leadership of the past.

Our current political parties thwart a lot of innovation and dialogue in Congress. And it is more-or-less unconstitutional. Party leadership is not supposed to be the gatekeeper for all legislation and amendments that can get a vote. Also, much of legislation must, under current rules, originate in Congressional Committees and be voted on through committees. These committees are not in the constitution. Even having "Majority Leaders" and such—parties controlling congress—is not in the Constitution. Subjects for a future book—it is the *structure* of our government and political system that needs to be re-evaluated and both modernized while re-establishing a legal foundation.

So, transitioning to the future with new leadership—completely new leadership that is not beholden to the same old way—is desperately needed for the U.S. to continue to lead the world in innovation.

---

[69] https://www.youtube.com/watch?v=YaAqnrpev44
[70] http://www.outsidethebeltway.com/huckabees_vertical_politics/

21
HISTORIC U.S.
ELECTION COMING?

Is it time for a breakthrough election? Is it even possible? When is the last time anything different has really happened in America?

Why do we go to the polls and vote? Do we do so on a case-by-case basis? Does the weather, or our business and/or personal schedule that day have an impact? How important is voting to you? Clearly, most voters are impacted by the 'stakes' of an election. In other words, not as many people vote in a primary as vote in a Presidential election. Many people that could vote, don't. Is it because they didn't register? Does registration hold back potential voters? Is it cynicism? Many currently believe their vote doesn't matter—that there isn't really a difference in their options.

So, when will we have a decisive election that shifts away from the Republicans and Democrats?

Eventually, it will have to happen. However, voters in America obviously play things close to the vest. Generally afraid of change. Generally afraid to rock the boat. Since America's first days it has been this way. It is, I suppose, ingrained in our voting DNA.

What does it take for a monumental election? Are there any examples?

Up until 1828, the Presidents of the United States were a continual procession of insiders. The Presidency was almost handed down from one titan to the next—most from the powerful state of Virginia.

List of the first 6 U.S. Presidents
George Washington (elected 1788, 1792)
John Adams (1796)

Thomas Jefferson (1800 and 1804)
James Madison (1808 and 1812)
James Monroe (1816 and 1820)
John Quincy Adams (1824)

It may not have *appeared* that all six of these Presidents were of the same elite cloth due to the contentious feud between the Federalists (George Washington and Alexander Hamilton) and the Democrat, Anti-Federalists (such as Thomas Jefferson). However out of these first six Presidents there was no straying outside those part and privy of the founding of the country.

Fourth, James Madison, was known as "the father of the Constitution." The 5th of these, James Monroe, was the "last founding father" to be President as he was present during much of the Constitution discussions.[71]

Jefferson was indeed dramatically different from George Washington on the issue of aristocratic, central government versus states' rights. However, in office, Jefferson tamed his sentiments and tracked the country not much off where it had been heading. For example, the Louisiana Purchase.

Some historians refer to this era as the "Virginia Dynasty." One of the first five—John Adams, only—was not from Virginia. The 6th President, John Quincy Adams was his son!

Something had to give.

And it nearly did, in 1824.

Along came Andrew Jackson. Not a shy one.

The Presidential election of 1824 was the frenzied height of this first round of insider-elite collusion in America.

In 1824, Andrew Jackson easily won the popular vote. He also solidly won the most electoral votes in the election.

However, his 99 electoral college votes were less than the 131 majority of electoral college votes necessary to win. And so, the Presidential election of 1824 would have to be decided by the U.S. House of Representatives.[72]

The House was led by the powerful Henry Clay of Kentucky. Clay coordinated what became known as the "corrupt bargain" to become Secretary of State in a John Quincy Adams administration. Adams had finished 2nd in the voting to Jackson, receiving just 30.9% of the popular vote (mostly from his neck of the woods, the Northeast).

However, with Clay pushing in the House, the son of America's 2nd President was inaugurated as the 6th President of the United States.[73]

---

[71] "The Last Founding Father" is the title of one of Harlon Giles Unger's books.

[72] https://en.wikipedia.org/wiki/United_States_presidential_election,_1824

[73] The 1824 Presidential election is the only election where the winner of the most electoral votes did not become the President. The 12th amendment was proposed in 1803 and ratified the following year to correct problems in the

According to historian H.W. Brands this era with "the anointing of successors by several presidents was one aspect of corruption" that "prevented ordinary people of America from controlling their government and their lives."[74]

The Presidency back then was not just handed down among a powerful succession of elites, but indeed even in the family. Sadly, not much different than it is today![75]

Third Parties in American History

Third parties in America?

Frankly, there isn't much history there! Probably to no real surprise.

Since the beginning of the United States of America there has never been a third party. An incredible, true statement.

1854 stands to date as perhaps the most incredible of all the elections in U.S. history. And the closest the U.S. ever came to a third party.

Sadly, since that time—over 160 years ago—there has been little remarkable in any and every election since.

The election of the 35th Congress in 1854 was the closest the U.S. ever came to having three parties in government. 43 seats out of the, then 234 in the House (18.4% of the seats). Nathaniel P. Banks led the American Party to the incredible win. The election of Congress in 1854 featured incredible disarray. The Republican Party was formed that year and won some seats.[76]

**1854 was an uprising
out of nowhere
for the United States of America.**

There have been movements and moments when a third party candidate captured national attention. In recent times, Ross Perot comes to mind. Ralph Nader to a lesser degree. And, George Wallace and the American

---

elections of 1796 and 1800. Under the 12th Amendment if no candidate earns a majority then the U.S. House of Representatives votes immediately for the winner. With the following important distinction: each state has 1 vote.

[74] *Andrew Jackson: His Life and Times* by H.W. Brands, pp 399

[75] George W. Bush, President elected in 2000 and 2004, as the son of George H.W. Bush, President after the election of 1988. In 2016 election, candidate Hillary Clinton the wife of the 42nd President, William Jefferson Clinton. So, this book is inspired in part because that type of elite dominance no doubt has too much of a grip on power now and does not serve enough of the people.

[76] https://en.wikipedia.org/wiki/United_States_House_of_Representatives_elections,_1854

Independent Party gathered 46 electoral college votes in 1968. That is the last time a third party Presidential candidate received any electoral college votes. Over 40 years ago!

It won't take all that much for a sweeping, sea change of an election. Given the low voter turnout, if ever even a slight amount of those people decides to vote sometime, look-out! It could be so unexpected how much things can change from one election to another. The power truly does reside with the people. And when the voters have their chance, I am sure make the most of the opportunity.

22

VOTERS ARE SMART

So… on the subject of elections… and voting.

I happen to believe voters are smart.

Voters inform themselves.

They weigh many factors. They vote with purpose. They vote with conscious.

Yes, voters can be manipulated. And we are. By deep pockets and a coordinated media. And, voters can be led. Or misled. Still, I am confident that those going to the polls do so sincerely; and they take their Constitutional right/privilege to vote very seriously.

Are there outliers? Sure. But as a general theory and as a mass of voters: people are voting with the best of intentions and effort. For a lot of voters, heading to the polls is tied to a specific reason—a certain issue, a friend running for office, financial interests—people vote with, and for a, reason. Right, some voters may not take in enough information, especially when it comes to all the races and issues on the ballot. Right, they might not know everything. For some voters it might be a little bit like an exam in college that you didn't fully prepare for. In fact, humbly speaking, that is a lot of the reality of voting. Wouldn't you like to know more if you could and/or had the time.

All that aside, most Americans go into the ballot box with as much information as they have been able to gather. They make an informed, educated and calculated decision. They take it seriously. They vote as responsibly as they can.

Voters are truly a lot <u>smarter</u> then given credit.

Why do some of us not vote? Should we all *have to* vote?

84

In one comparison, voting is seen as a right just like owning a gun is a right. Just because you can own a gun doesn't mean you have to.[77] Whether you subscribe to a notion like that, people *should* vote. Make a commitment to vote. 9 times out of 10 the right answer is to vote. Excuses such as 'my vote doesn't matter' and the electoral college means my vote is not that important. None of that really matters. All the numbers get reported. The percentages people win by make a difference. Your vote may not decide things in a state but in counting the national total and percentages it can have an impact.

At the same time, people should not feel guilty for not voting. Right now, the amount of corporate/banker money involved does mean that are choices are sometimes false and nothing is going to change.

So, those staying home are staying home for a reason.

Those that don't vote usually do so out of respect of the ballot. That they have been too busy and don't feel informed enough to make a decision.

Sometimes they don't vote. For a reason. Voters are smart though. There are times to maybe stay home. If you don't have a dog in the fight. For example, property taxes. One time a property tax vote for funding schools with tax revenue from a property tax. If you don't own a home or property, maybe it's not yours. And a colleague told me they were staying home and not voting because they didn't own a house. I can respect that.

Voter turnout even in presidential elections is at or below 60%. In an off election it can be below 40%. Voters have a lack of trust in *all* politicians. And voters are definitely indicating they don't like the choices and they don't believe voting makes a difference. That needs to change! We need new parties, and big changes to ballot access and vote counting.

A lot goes into why we vote. What issues are at stake that election? Relationship to candidates. Identity with, understanding and/or comfort with a candidate. Accepting a candidate—in other words bending to what we can.

Can we get more people to vote?

The important thing is people should *want* to vote. They should like their options. We don't have that. This is another way in which voters are smart. Some do see it as two of the same options so why vote until something really changes. So, even if it is a 'throw their hands up, there is no difference' type of staying home and refusing to vote; that, in itself, is a calculated, thought-out position.

Solutions, such as mandatory voting is not necessary. Better candidates and a more open system where real people can run is needed. People will vote when there is a reason. More options, and better options, will increase

---

[77] http://qpolitical.com/24-hours-after-last-nights-debate-mike-rowe-makes-a-huge-confession-on-what-he-see-wrong-with-this-election/

voter participation.

Voters are not stupid. In fact, voters are quite smart. Think about the daily routine items in our lives. We drive cars. A 3,000 lb. object going 55 miles per hour, whizzing by other cars, day after day. They are staying home for a reason. There needs to be some big changes and new faces, with loftier goals and stronger character and potential. And, with the right messages, the voters will be showing up. It has been corporate/banker candidate A vs corporate/banker candidate B for a while now.

Voting is not all that complicated. People may not like the outcome. Intellectuals and pundits may sneer at the results. However, voters *are* indeed smart. They do know what they are doing. Voters listen. Voters read. Voters have their own thoughts and opinions. And, voters have their own, unique experiences. And they express this at the ballot box. All of this makes for an informed decision.

We could help more people vote by changing some aspects of election day. We have started down this road with more, and easier, absentee ballot options. Two voting days? Longer voting hours? What do the establishment powers have to lose by enabling more people to get to the polls and cast a vote?

23
WORDS AND MEANING

Political issues can be quite difficult to talk about and the same word can either a) have different meanings to different people and/or b) heighten people's emotions simply by hearing the word.

The choice of a word can have a crucially different interpretation in your mind and there's.

The Same Word:
Different meanings from one person to the next
While conjuring varying emotions and feelings

What our own meaning of a word is varies.

Also, how we feel when we hear a word differs.

Just hearing a certain word can set some people off.

Two people (Jackie and Tom), that agree on a topic, let's say 'capitalism' may have a) completely different reasons why they support capitalism; and, it is also entirely possible that b) capitalism means different things to each of them. They are supporting the same word, but it is different.

For example, Jackie is more supportive of the, let's say, 'ruthless' type of capitalism that everyone gets their just rewards of hard work and effort whereas Tom does not associate as much with that aspect of capitalism; for Tom it is that capitalism affords freedoms to live the way (and work the job) that you want to.

A person might even be entirely flat out wrong about the meaning of the word. But it is how they see it. The point is recognizing the effects of words used on communication with others. It most definitely impacts our ability to get along.

We may define the same exact word a bit differently in our heads.

And beyond that, hearing and reading words can bring out emotions. To a liberal, the word "liberal" is positive. That means hearing the word puts you in a relaxed state, or a good mood. To a conservative, the word "liberal" can conjure up bad feelings and negative emotions. So, the use of the same word could put one person at ease while causing another to cringe up.

Consider so many loaded words: capitalism, globalism, socialism, etc. These words all mean different things to different people. The words take on different meanings in different contexts. We are unlikely to define our way into a better future. We must confront each other head on with honest and frank dialogue.

Some might say words are literally losing some meaning.[78]

It is difficult, or not fair, to define people according to a political term. Conservative. Republican. Liberal. Democrat. For one thing, there are shades of allegiance, degrees of how liberal, conservative, Republican and/or Democrat any of us are. More than that, each of these words mean different things to different people. If we call someone a liberal, your definition of a liberal and mine are different. So, as a society, we need to look harder and dig deeper. And dialogue longer and more thoroughly.

---

[78] Including legendary film director Martin Scorsese in a 2016 interview http://www.independent.co.uk/arts-entertainment/films/news/martin-scorsese-silence-new-films-disposable-over-saturation-press-conference-a7471996.html

24
TRIANGLE OF DISCUSSION

How can we find some common understanding?

What is the path forward?

How can we come to agreement? Amid so much political tension.

One path to compromise is to view conversation on tough topics as a dialogue. With a starting point. And an ending point.

Our political positions are journeys that we arrive to. And conversations should be followed where they can take us. And/or enjoyed while we are in them. In the moment.

I think of a triangle. And I use this concept in sales.

My conversations to close a sale start at the base of a triangle. With a line between me and the person(s) I am talking to. The line representing the difference between me hoping they will buy the product and a customer on the other side looking to buy should it be helpful and beneficial to their business... Or the line can represent differences in opinions. And differences in understanding.

There is an initial gap between you and your friend when discussing a particular political issue (the line shown below).

You ●————————● Friend

That gap in mutual understanding illustrated as you on one side of the base of the triangle and your potential new colleague at the other end of the base of the triangle.

At the beginning of the conversation your understandings may not align. Through the conversation you both move up the triangle to the point where your understanding is now aligned. The conversation is a back-and-forth up the triangle, increasingly toward mutual understanding.

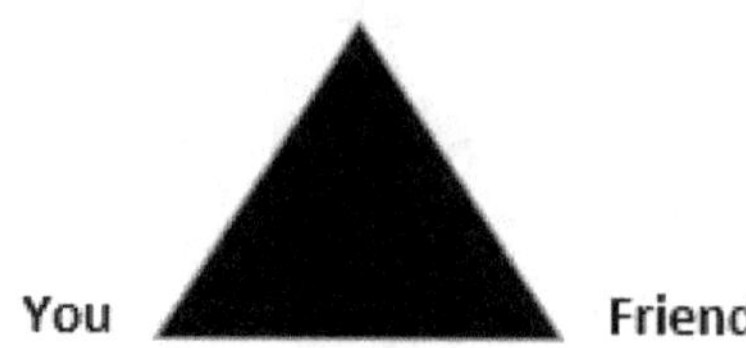

The goal is to arrive at the top of the triangle with a mutual understanding. So, this doesn't mean having to agree on everything. Maybe you find agreement. Maybe you 'agree-to-disagree.'

This is a path to working with people you never thought you could agree with. Bill Clinton talked about triangulation. The triangulation of Bill Clinton and Tony Blair was more macro in seeking a new way to look at a specific piece of legislation that could find a compromise among all the representatives. The point of the triangle here is a little more about *one conversation* starting from an unknown point (which may be of more-or-less agreement) and moving the conversation along.

The result may be as simple as agreeing on 1 out of 10 items. Well, at least on that 1 issue you arrived together at the top of the triangle with a mutual understanding. Or, even if you totally disagree on every political issue you discussed, you might still say you arrived at the top of the triangle because you at least can understand where they are coming from.

Press. "Ok, so on the subject of _____, can you explain that a little more" "can we talk about ___ a little further?" "What did you mean when you said ___". Build toward a common understanding. So, it can be helpful to look at your conversation as a triangle. You start out the conversation at the bottom of the triangle. And work your way up.

If it all is as bad as it could be. Say, you can't even 'agree-to-disagree;' you fume thinking about their politics. With a triangle in mind, and conversation as a journey, a sidebar element of the conversation—something about their family, or job/education or current circumstances, interests—probably there can always be *something* you can take away as a positive.

Let's talk about that. Ask one more question. "Oh, interesting... so you mean" or "why is that," "tell me more" "what do you mean by _____?" What do you mean when you say ___? Can you describe what ___ means to you?

Can you tell me more about that?

Can you say more about that? This is a great way to 1) keep the conversation flowing and, more importantly 2) ensure mutual understanding. Look you really want to know and see exactly what they mean and exactly what they are thinking. Like a kid: When? How? Why? What? Where?

Humble yourself. Be curious. These are ways to help you listen more. And listening builds understanding.

Elementary?

Perhaps. But politics in America has come to this. The future is not through ideological blindness or locking people out. We *have to* be able to work with everyone.

I have found a great quote relevant for today's times:

> "Retain, if you will, a fixed political opinion, yet do not parade it upon all occasions, and, above all, do not endeavor to force others to agree with you. Listen calmly to their ideas upon the same subjects, and if you cannot agree, differ politely, and while your opponent may set you down as a bad politician, let him be obliged to admit that you are a gentleman."
>
> – from Cecil B. Hartley's *A Gentleman's Guide to Etiquette*

25

COKE OR PEPSI?

The greater philosopher and political theorist, Snoop Dogg, or Snoop Doggy Dog, lol; perhaps he said it best.

"Just chill, til the next episode?"[79]

When you meet someone and start talking about movies, wines or beers—if they don't like the same ones you do does that get us riled up? Sometimes you like the same things. Other times you don't.

It *can* be similar with political issues too.

Pro-choice or pro-life? We each come to the issue with different life experiences and different values.

Let's make our political analysis more like our real, day-to-day life. You can be friends with your neighbor without dabbing in each's others politics. You can go over to your aunt or cousin's house, hang out, watch some football, knit, eat dinner—what have you—and not talk politics. Could be diametrically opposed to each other. We *can* get along. And we can talk a lot more than we do. If we just cut each other people some slack. Hey, so they don't agree with you on a political question. So what.

We are all very unique!

Which is a good thing. We only need to give ourselves this credit. And back off from each other a little bit.

Do you like Coca-Cola or ice tea? What is your opinion on abortion? Ok, yes, they *are* absolutely *totally* different topics… with much bigger implications

---

[79] https://youtu.be/MZ_ILWwx9Rw?t=3m25s

in society. However, the general point is: guess what? We are different! It can come as no surprise in politics just as it does with other things.

We can lighten up a little in politics.

Doesn't mean disengage from politics. Doesn't mean moderate your own opinions.

We *attribute* and *assign* too much negativity to an opposing political party, without addressing the fundamental reality that you interact daily on an individual level with such people.

We need to give each other space to talk and vote based on different beliefs. The reasons why others hold a certain perspective can at least be respected, if not interesting.

Hopefully, we are getting close to "peak polarization" political opinion (as some people are now calling it).[80] Just need to change our perspective and mindset on other people's politics.

Maybe different politicians (or one of their speeches) are like different movies. Sometimes there are certain movies that we all like. Other times, two people watch a movie and have completely different opinions about it. Timing is part of that. I watched the movie first. I liked it. I told you to go see it because it's really good. You see it the next day. At that time, you weren't in the mood for that type of movie. And, you end up not liking it. Your heightened expectations, based on my positive comments, probably played a role. It didn't live up to the hype, so to speak. If we are all geared up to see an awesome movie and then find it to be anything less than awesome, we express disappointment.

Political Interpretation

There are art related factors. It is not all science. It is what *you* see; what *you* hear? And, what resonates with you. other people may not see the speech you saw. Other people don't experience it the way you do. It doesn't exactly impact all of us the same. Like music. And a big song. A certain rift. Sometimes it grabs us all. Movies like *Titanic*. And it is ever changing. Even from day to day. You listen to that favorite song over and over again. And then suddenly it is old. There could be an issue that if you scored the day before it may not be the biggest, yet in the speech that day, the candidate you just connected with them and made a general impression that may last.

The key here is self-realization.

---

[80] http://nymag.com/daily/intelligencer/2017/05/in-the-trump-era-america-is-racing-toward-peak-polarization.html and
https://www.seattletimes.com/seattle-news/politics/in-seattle-is-it-now-taboo-to-be-friends-with-a-republican/.

And with that to realize we are all like that. To cut people some slack.

You have your hardline views and feel, however, that you appreciate all other people. So, assume that's how other people are as well.

A lot of the animosity is media driven. Do we need to tune out a little? So that we can be more in the moment and present with the individuals with us. Understanding why. Or at least appreciating that they are different; just like you are different.

26

THE JOURNEY:
ARRIVING AT YOUR
POLITICAL POSITIONS

We all are far more independently minded then our ultimate positions demonstrate. We *arrive* at our political positions. People look at us for the condition we are in when we arrive; without ever asking about the journey.

Why do we have that view?

Unique events happen to each of us, independently. Sometimes very personal and/or triggering events that make for hardline stands on an issue. Other times, a random conversation or chance encounter here-and-there that adds nuance to our viewpoint.

Why does the person you are talking to believe as they do? What is their *thought process*? Why does the person that you totally disagree with believe as they do? There is more to the story then simply: *what* do they believe? We focus so much on *what* people believe and where they stand... today. And we need to understand how we all form our opinions along the way. Based on what we perceive... and think... and experience. Can we spend more time trying to get to know each other?

We *arrive* at our political viewpoints
Every one of us, had a journey
to our positions on issues.

Can we spend more time trying to understand where people are coming from? Unique events happen to each of us along the way of life.

95

The strange thing is that we might even be wrong. Like your Uncle Jerry. But, you know where Uncle Jerry stands. He tells you all about *why* he insists on being wrong. Well, Jerry can go vote. And all of us have a little more 'Uncle Jerry' in us than we might want to admit. I don't know everything. You don't know everything. Certainly, when it comes to some political question. We gather the information that we can, and we make an informed decision. Some of us are better communicators… better negotiators… better at arguing. Even better educated. Don't mistake that for being right. And, that… well, that can take us into philosophical discussions about majority rule.

Anyway, let's get to know the individual. The person.

And know why.

Then we can all begin to understand.

There may be legitimate reasons why they believe as they do. And even if you will never agree, talking in person, is going to be a better alternative.

Let's show some appreciation for their perspective—their journey. Try to get inside that trip and listen to how they arrived where they are today. Give people some space. Let's be different. You can often learn a lot from people you disagree with. Sometimes it only serves to sharpen your views. Other times it changes them. All conversations have the potential to be deeply rewarding if we just give some space. And keep an open mind. Challenge your own opinions.

We are all Independents

Ultimately, we are all independents. And that is even the out there liberal and the hard-right conservative. And, the centrist too.

Those that you most agree with. Even your agreements are far more different than you can appreciate. Understanding that can build more trust.

**Whether we solidly align with a third party…
or one of the establishment parties…
each of us is still at the end of the day
an independent.**

None of stand for everything on a party platform. Any of us are liable to leave a party at any moment.

Even more precisely, every one of us is an independent in that we have unique opinions. Sometimes in politics we start to not trust those closest to us; because we know them too well. There *are* differences (well, maybe you have one "political soulmate" or "political twin" out there, lol).

All of us come at events from different perspectives.

We all hear different things. We have different educations. Different jobs. Different co-workers. Different news sources. Different levels of interest in the news altogether. We could agree on an issue but not agree for the same reasons. I might be very pro-life because of my religion. Another might not be religious at all but had a relative that had a bad experience and did scientific investigation to arrive at a similar believe that life begins at conception.

Appreciate Our Differences

We need to appreciate all perspectives. We are all different. So what!? That is a good thing.

Sunday morning. Some of us wake up and go get a Starbucks latte and read the paper. Some of us don't wake up on Sunday morning—stayed up too late the night before—and then meet up with some old friends for brunch. Some of us go out for a jog. Some pick up where they left off on a project they are working on—writing a book, trying to solve a scientific problem, fixing something in the garage.

Many of us dress up nice on Sunday morning, go to Church and pray with our family, friends and congregation. Some of us head out in our pickup truck to fish, or hunt. Some of us are at the golf course. Some of us are trying a new recipe in the kitchen while watching a TV show.

We have lost the ability for 'civil discourse.' You could say it started with TV talk shows and news. But as Mobile Archbishop Thomas J. Rodi says "civil discourse appears to be less and less valued in our society" at-large.[81] We have become, as a society, a TV show shouting match. Social media for example, has a lot of one-sided shouting. Many areas in our lives could benefit from conversation and discussion.

How do we turn this around? Well, say you are talking with someone and they may say something you know is wrong. Pause. Don't stop them at that moment. Listen to their full message. There is always time to counter. It could even be the next day. "Hey, John, I was thinking about what you said yesterday and from what I have seen that one point about x is not correct. Have you seen a book called y? It explains what I have found to be the case." And, if you listen long enough, sometimes you find they bring their point full circle and your initial reaction on one aspect of what they are saying isn't the full picture.

Other times they are wrong. Or, you think they are wrong. At least show some respect for perspectives you disagree with. Doesn't mean you have to agree and certainly doesn't mean you condone their view. Simply find a good way to approach a counterpoint. You don't have to jump down the person's throat the first word you hear that sets you off. Pause. Let them talk. It is not a game of 'gotcha.' A lot of times with liberal media it is about attacking the person. Bush Katrina, etc. Instead of listening until you hear the word you

---

[81] Civil discourse seems to be less and less valued, *The Catholic Week*, September 29, 2017, Pp 3.

disagree with or the point that sets you off into a reaction, why not listen for the word you agree on.

**Instead of listening for the word or thing
you *disagree* with
Wait and pick out something you agree on.
See where that takes your conversation!**

Why not listen for the one word where you can say 'oh, I agree with that.' See where *that* approach takes our conversations.

Keep an open mind, challenge yourself as much as others

Critical thinking. All of us. Everything read, heard or even seen isn't always what we think it is. Sometimes we are hoping to hear what we want to hear and that *becomes* what we heard even when that isn't what was *said*. The meaning of words enters into this too. Because you can jump on the word that was said, but before jumping too much, do you understand that person's real intent, and their own meaning of that word? In other words, technically they may have said that word, but it doesn't mean what *you* think it means. And, I don't mean any of this in a 'gotcha' sense either. Or a trickery sense. You don't get to mean something when you say it. And then *act* like you meant something different later. All as part of a game. That immaturity must stop.

In my own interpretation, we as individuals should repeatedly re-examine our own viewpoints. Open-mindedness to other possibilities, in my view, is the critical element of an open society. Open-mindedness helps to harmonize changes in society.

And, fundamental to an open mind is **fallibility**. Recognizing we make mistakes. That we make mistakes means... that some of *our own* views may be flawed. Or *wrong*. Our own view, as right as we believe it to be—is not always correct. With that admission—both to ourselves, and to others in politics and discussion—breeds the humility that can sow trust.

Give Each Other Space

More than anything, we need to be free to think. We need to be free to talk. If we can learn to listen. If we can learn to tolerate what others might say, we can move forward as well as begin to heal. Might *say*. *Say*. This is like Allen Iverson's viral video of his "Practice" press conference remarks. We are not talking about what people *do*. Can we first simply let others *talk*?

Tantrums at UC Berkeley over conservatives coming to the campus to speak is ridiculous.

For the freedom of speech (which, by the way, was instituted in the founding of the country as a First Amendment right), we need listeners.

That is, for those that speak: there is an audience.

Any of us should be listeners. We need to be better, and good, listeners.

So, this theme of increasing our own openness to others. Committing to dialogue and listen to others you may not agree with. That is one of the big themes of overcoming the odds.

27

FINDING SOLUTIONS;
AND CONCLUDING REMARKS

We haven't even scratched the surface of understanding each other's politics. Each of our politics is so much more complex than conventional wisdom suggests. We know it about ourselves—the nuance of *our own* views. Now we just need to credit each other and appreciate each other for the political viewpoints we arrive at.

The fourth element of a person's views on a particular political issue is: **how would you *solve* the issue**? So, you are an environmentalist; and an ardent 10 out of 10 on the scale too. Plus, it is your most important issue. That said, how would you solve the issue? Do you think it must be resolved by the federal government and adopted as a national law? Do you think global agreements and essentially world government are necessary to impose the solution? Or, can it be a state-by-state solution? Or even local? Or left to the free market to work it out with no government involvement?

Is it so important that everyone must bend to your view? Some issues *are* that important to some voters. For example, for a conservative pro-life proponent, the life of a baby is at stake and therefore every life of a fetus must be protected.

Consider marijuana legalization and so-called "sanctuary cities." Liberals are fine to completely flaunt federal laws and have local and state-wide solutions on these issues. And then, when it comes to marriages and baking cakes they want federal courts imposing decisions on the nation. Same could be said for some gun rights proponents. If they can carry their gun in some states, why can't they carry it in other states?

You can start to see how complex perspectives on the *solutions* to issues can become. And when you try to add this into understanding the totality of what a voter's politics are, well your head can start to spin. You end up with multiple dimensions to analyze; adding layers of complexity—"quantum politics."

It can be more easily analyzed on an issue-by-issue basis. And it could be a game changer in-and-of-itself to see where people come out. Some big-time issues might be easily solved if you start to find out how voters want them solved. That's the simple in "quantum politics." You mean it is as easy as asking people how they want a particular issue solved?

What if on a particular 50/50 social issue,
85% of the people say
leave decisions about it to the states?
That could sure simplify a path forward.

How would you solve the issue you are being asked about?

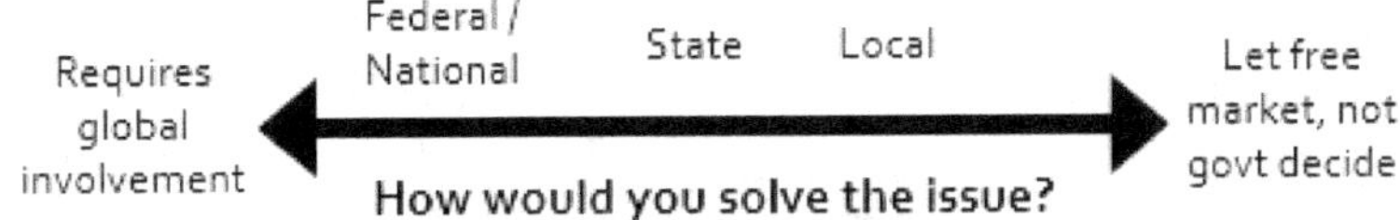

If we start asking voters how would you solve the issue it might make it a lot easier to come up with the right solutions.

So, this is where the conversation needs to go for the future of effective politics. Upping the game on left-right politics.

Taking our analysis up a level. Looking at politics in totally new ways.

Finding better ways to understand the particulars about our politics.

Left-right politics pigeon holes us. We have a lot more potential!

Could even the solutions be said to wrap around? For example, could there be a global "protocol" that enables local variation and/or free market competition and non-government outcomes?

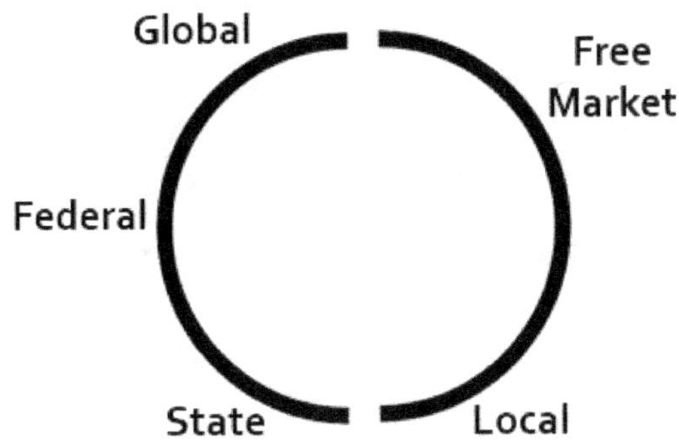

The complexity becomes apparent here when considering multinational corporations and banks. They could either highlight a divide between what is a truly "free market" (with small businesses and competition) and what is "crony capitalism" (abusing lobbyist power to right all laws in their own favor). Or corporations could represent how certain people want different solutions from issue to issue—to have it both ways too. Corporations want to be able to have global organizations that ensure they can do business anywhere in the world, while at the same-time they might want no government involvement on particular aspects of environmental issues. And that delves into sub-questions because corporations are more than willing to push hard for "carbon credits" and "cap-and-trade" schemes that make it difficult for smaller competitors (thus seemingly sounding like environmentalists); while at the same-time turning a blind-eye to the pollution they are causing in local rivers.

The "political circle" is one way for us to start looking at politics differently. Starting with this simple bending of the traditional left-right line. Helping to open minds to new possibilities and alternative alignments.

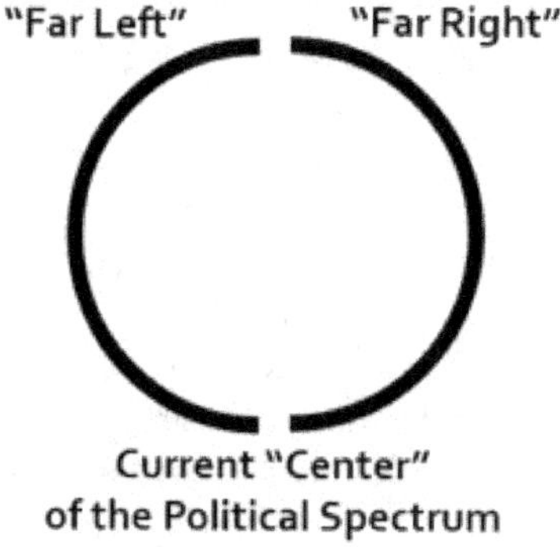

In America, we have always innovated. Always paved a new way. We can spin this circle a different way.

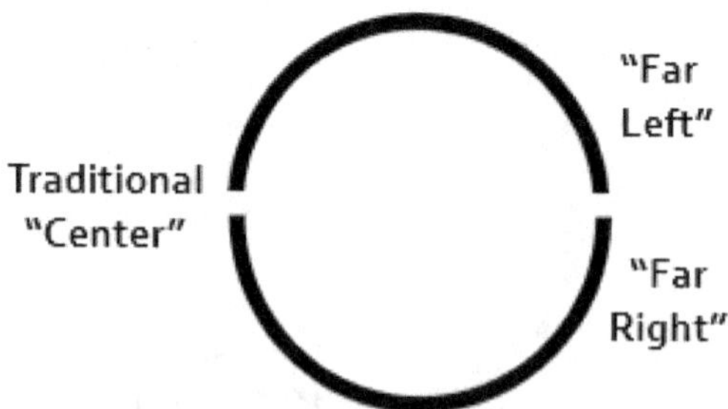

Then, you can add various 'differentiators' to the circle. Because what is the right way to illustrate the nature of the divided between liberal and conservative?

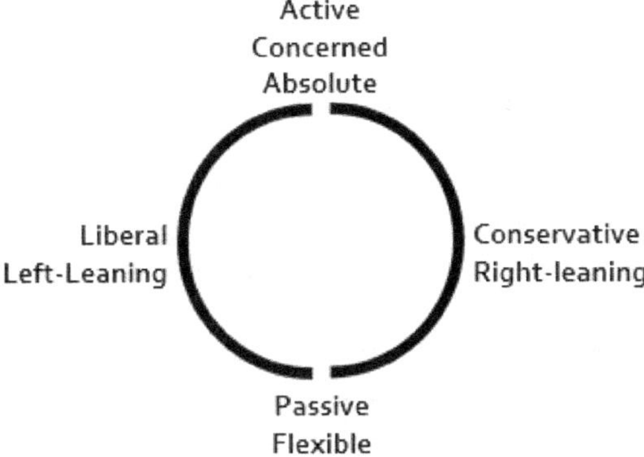

This next one is a same twist; however, lining up left and right based on how much they want the solutions imposed nationally versus how libertarian the person is in truly being tolerant that other parts of the country could take their own approach. Recall in Chapter 10 the ISideWith.com chart that places "personal freedom" near liberal viewpoints and "legislative morality" near conservative viewpoints. When the reality is that there are liberals that want their viewpoints imposed and conservatives that want their own state or local difference and could care less about another state. So, these types of distinctions are important to discover.

Surveys built to uncover where our politics are on circles such as this, could help two colleagues to better understand each other, or people getting together for a roundtable discussion to have original insights, and deeper understandings of what the others attending believe.

<u>Forming</u> Opinions,
Arriving at Political Viewpoints

We know it about ourselves. We give ourselves credit for being nuanced and balanced. We believe we can, and do, objectively call it all. Many of us believe we have the answers.

Now if only we can recognize that about each other. The person you totally disagree with, the people (constituency) you think has it all wrong… *they* think they are right. *And,* they are pretty sure about it. They have it all rationalized a different way.

And that can bring us all full circle.

Maybe you are wrong. And they are right.

Sometimes.

And vice versa.

Or, maybe we could at least talk it all through together. If only we start by recognizing who we are talking about has it together in their head a different way. Just like us.

Let's put this another way…

We don't just *have* a position on an issue.

We **form** our positions.

We form them via a set of different experiences; different circumstances; different information sources. And even when we hear the same speeches and hear the same words, we interpret it all a little differently.

Our answers to where we stand on important political issues are **formed in a journey**. We ***arrive*** at our positions. We don't just have an answer. And a word for a person to jump on to win an argument.

It is all more nuanced. A lot of it can't just be summed up with a nice bow on top. Why? Why do they believe what they believe?

That is the message for this book.

To open our minds to look at politics more expansively.

To open our politics to new potentials and possibilities.

Enabling bold new combinations, richer discussions… and move us along toward implementation of the innovative solutions we are most capable of.

Where Next?

The grand aim of this book is to open minds and possibilities. The 21st Century is likely to be more different from the 20th Century than this past 100 years was from the 1800's. And for America to continue being at the forefront of innovation, bold and dynamic approaches to our politics and our system of government must be assessed, confronted and adopted.

We need new politicians that can keep up. Now!

I am tired of both parties. They are both corrupt. They are both in it for themselves—in it for the money, their donors, big banks and mega corporations. I don't support the self-serving way. Are self-serving politicians nice people? Sure. And, so are a lot of people. But, we have lost our way in America. Call it 'government of-the-money, by -the-money, for-the-money.'

Our constitution was written to be state-focused, but we have become totally federalized. We have unaccountable judges—placed on the Supreme Court for life-long terms. Ridiculous. We have a federal government that is so big that Washington, DC is the richest city in the country—7 of the top 10 richest counties in the U.S. are suburbs of the nation's capital. We have a federal debt of $20 trillion! A Federal Reserve that gets to counterfeit money for big banks. None of this was intended by the founders.[8283]

Today we have career politicians—and it is getting old. Democrats *and* Republicans support this. Senators for 30 years. 40 years. That is ridiculous. President is limited to two, 4-year terms; 8 years in office. The representatives vote for a term limit for President but not themselves.

<u>Combined House and Senate
Time in Washington DC</u>[84]
John Dingell: 59 years (retired)
Robert Byrd: 57 years (died in office)
Thad Cochran: 45 years (present)
Don Young: 44 years (present)
Patrick Leahy: 43 years (present)
Chuck Grassley: 43 years (present)
Ed Markey: 41 years (present)
Orrin Hatch: 41 years (present)

---

[82] One founding father that liked centralized control was Alexander Hamilton. Despite his rosy portrayals lately (typical redefining of history by liberal establishment) Hamilton was the ultimate loyalist to the British monarchy.

[83] I believe a lot of problems could be better solved left to state-to-state differences. Liberals have no problem approving, for example, marijuana and sanctuary cities in their states; so there should also be conservative states allowed to have different views on abortion and marriage.

[84] Selected examples via https://en.wikipedia.org/wiki/List_of_members_of_the_United_States_Congre ss_by_longevity_of_service

59 years in office? That really happened. Four current Senators that have been in Washington, DC over 41 years—and counting! These are *some* selected examples—showing the 2 longest ever as well as several of the longest *currently* serving. It is ridiculous! Over 40 years in Washington, DC. It is not supposed to be a career. This is among the biggest problems: bringing in fresh energy.

Our current establishment—walking the halls of Congress for 30-40 years—is the complete opposite of the right mentality.

Retire. Move along.
Plenty of great people that can serve!

We need better people in power. We need politicians that want to represent the people; finding the best solutions outside of the influence of party and donors.

It is a structural problem. The Democrats and Republicans have institutionalized seniority into their power structures such that no one wants their representative to lose the power they have accumulated by time in office. We will fall behind big time if we cannot get fresh, new representatives in Washington. It goes beyond voting and it is one of the reasons why in the chapter on "**future political parties**" one of the defining characteristics of a successful future party is likely to be their rules and process, in how they reward and determine leadership.

Responsibility for all of this does in a good part of the deal, rest with the population and citizens. We *do* get to vote for these people; or someone else. It is really *our* choice. And our power.

Vote for someone different!

Congressional approval ratings are below 20%. Terrible! Yet, we vote the same people in—over and over. At the end of the day it is us; we, the people, are to blame. There are elections in the House every 2 years. Every 2 years we could change over the entire House.

Sadly, that is complacency. The people are complacent. Led; and misled.

There needs to be an awakening.

I don't want to vote for another Democrat. Ever. And I don't want to vote for another Republican either!

So, I am starting to do whatever I can for a new direction.

It has been the same two parties for far, far too long.

It is hard to believe that since the time of the Civil War there have only been the same two political parties. It is hard to believe that no other party has so much as even gained hardly any traction. At some point this will have to change. One way or the other. In other words, if we don't soon see some more political diversity, the United States of America may see massive movements toward changing or ending the Constitution and/or secession.

The fact of no other party since the Civil War is a strong indication of the **magnitude of shift that will be necessary**.

Amid success, the tendency is to stagnate. Our establishment's primary goals are to protect their own interests—stifling innovation. And, it is not only a federal issue—local politicians, state politicians also share in this problem of establishment corruption.

We need some fresh parties. **Completely different faces**—a new type of leader. **Serving the people**; and **facilitating discussion** and implementation of new ideas—with **bold, innovative solutions**.

Standing Strong, yet Light and Flexible

Hagia Sophia, in Istanbul, is an incredible feat of engineering—completed 1500 years ago in the 6th Century. It's one of the largest buildings in the world; still standing impressively today. Once inside, visitors gaze up 182 feet at one of the largest domes on the planet. Currently a museum, previously a Mosque and initially built as a Christian Church, the imposing structure is also remarkable for being built amid one of the largest earthquake zones on earth.[85]

How strong was the construction?

Ironically, recent investigation discovers that key aspects of the construction feature *light* materials and *flexible design elements*.[86] It is these light and flexible elements that give the building its strength—providing slight 'give' under stress that prevents a break.

Can it be with our politics? Take each other lightly. Be flexible to find areas of agreement. Conservatives are right about some things. Liberals are right about some things. And, wrong too. You aren't always right.

The imposing, massive building *stands*, though light and flexible. In other words, it does not mean you have to leave your opinions at the door. In fact, we should be more comfortable to share our real beliefs if we know others can accept hearing it. Don't go quiet on what you believe to prove your tolerance.

Different Strokes for Different Folks

---

[85] https://en.wikipedia.org/wiki/Hagia_Sophia
[86] https://hagiasophiaturkey.com/building-materials-hagia-sophia/

We all have a role to play. There is no correct way to be involved in politics. There are people that are set on an issue. Passionate about it. There is no debate about it with them. And, you know what, that's great. Whatever their position is. Thank God we have some passionate people out there! They might have a great idea about it. Or they might be ahead of the population on their view. Or, yes, maybe they *are* off their rocker and need to calm down.

Some people are calm negotiators, listening, facilitating compromise. And we need that. We also need leaders that can rise above and not be afraid to speak their mind and take bold actions. There is a time for it all. Lots of ingredients in good gumbo.

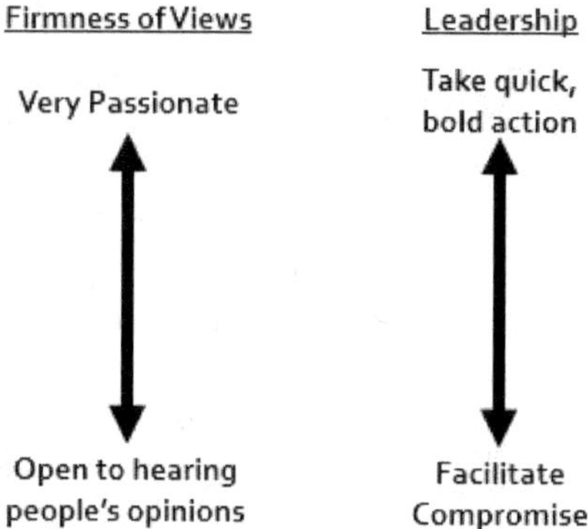

Respecting each other. A simple concept. Many connotations over the years. Aretha Franklin's song, R.E.S.P.E.C.T, popularized the term amid the Civil Rights era of the 1960's. I use it more to signify on an individual-to-individual basis.

Really, a song's lyrics are a good place to jump off. Some want to say this is now "the feminist anthem" and of course this song has a certain meaning for African-Americans through the years. The song can be as deep, philosophical and political as anyone wants to make it out to be. And, at the same time, it can just be a catchy tune to others. And, here, in *this book*, it's just a simple metaphor for each other. Is someone talking some politics? Whatever is coming out of their mouth…. whatever those words are entering your ears and affecting your brain and emotions… let's have a little respect. That's all.

Silent and listen. Both words use the same exact letters. Can we talk to new people? Can we listen to alternative viewpoints?

We need to up our game. Understand each other better. Delve deeper into our politics.

Step back—look at each other one issue at a time, try to better understand each other, have much deeper conversations and push ourselves to much better outcomes. Value our differences.

**If we can recognize, in ourselves,
the wide variations in our views from issue to issue
(sometimes even inconsistent).
And the nuances to our own
strongly held political opinions,
we should then be able to
acknowledge it exists in others.**

Further, it is not about trying to manipulate others to our point of view. In recent years liberals have touted books like *Nudge* and *Rules for Radicals*. That will not be the politics of the future. Yes, you need to fight for what you believe in. But the ultimate victory is *not* in deception. And it is *not* in dirty tactics. The future will be love and appreciation. Talk. Freedom. A dynamism that borders on anarchy. A future of win-win-win solutions.

If we have respect for other people, then we invite them to become free to express their true selves. And we get closer to really making life better. Much better political results when we can have truer conversations.

When we can work with new people. Fresh ideas and new approaches are possible. At a more basic level, the people will be set free. To speak our hearts and true minds. To vote more faithfully to our core values.

The Political Circle and a New Era of Quantum Politics

Political Circle
Quantum Politics
The left-right spectrum is so limiting.
It creates stereotypes. It creates division. It creates a divide.
And it creates a "center" that thinks they rise above it all.
One takeaway regarding the current definition of centrists as the middle of the left-right political spectrum is that there is only one center. The political circle changes that. Gone is the "far left" and the "far right."
How many different combinations of people could get together to form a consensus? It is not just the people in the center. The center is what we have been taught. The center dominates our political frame of reference. However, as a math question we know there are a lot of different possibilities for the people in a room to get together and form a consensus. If we do not think of party or labels theoretically any of us could talk with one another. And, people you may think are your political enemy may in fact be a possible partner in developing a win-win solution that makes life better for all of us.

That is the essence of the political circle. There is no longer just one center. Anywhere along the 'political circle' can be a center. There are infinite centers. Any of us could be the center. If that is our purpose. We don't all need to moderate. But if you can listen and facilitate the point is don't think you need to be in some mythical center between right and left to do it.

Mathematically, the complexity in our politics is introduced by the myriad of issues, and sub-questions. And when you try to break this down into an equation to be solved you quickly realize it is impossible to fit all people along a spectrum. It is as complex as the many ways of mathematics—trig, calculus, geometry, arithmetic. It can be graphed in lines—horizontal and vertical, diagonal. Circles, triangles, cylinders, dimensions.

The world's smartest scientists have been engaged throughout the history of humanity to frame the rules of our universe—from Newton's laws of motion and gravity to Einstein's relativity; and now quantum mechanics. Yet, those theories are different. Not really unified. And for 100 years, with the greatest minds searching for answers—using the best technology—the only thing we are concluding now is that "reality is not what it seems" and "something still eludes us."[87] Both are right. Light is sometimes a wave and sometimes a particle. Modern science is filled with contradictions. And this is the future of politics—the "quantum era" of politics—when we 'discover' and utilize the fact that we are all right about this part or that part. We all have positives to contribute.

What's Your Favorite Kind of Pizza?

We are on a collision course heading in the opposite and wrong direction. For so many reasons, there is a trend toward intensification of political perspectives—call it hyper politics. Part of it is definitely the media. The media fires up emotions and stokes divide. All kinds of websites have made it easier for us to find those that we most closely identify with. But it is all going to change for the better.

Calling someone liberal or conservative. That is not enough. Right or left. That doesn't say much either. Not even really slivers of the story. Democrat or Republican, centrists or extremist it is all in what you hear and what those words mean to you and to them.

In all parts of life, we have lots of differences
So, we should expect our politics are as unique

---

[87] *Reality is Not What It Seems*, Carlo Rovelli, 2014. Reference to title and quote from page 148.

Religions: Even within Christianity so many denominations
Singers (sopranos, etc.), piano players, guitarists, drummers
Types of food we like
Diets that we follow
Songs that we like
Favorite movies
Hobbies
Jobs that we prefer to work
Favorite subject in school
Types of books we like to read (if we like to read at all)
Favorite beverage
Favorite kinds of candy

Do you like pizza? What kind of milk do you prefer to drink? Putting meat on the grill? Vegetarian? Vegan? Ice cream? Juicing? Healthy foods only? Cheese or no cheese? How much do we like chocolate? 0 to 10?

If we like a particular song, or band, is it because of the people we were with when listening to it (out with someone special, seeing them live in concert, etc.).

And so it should be with politics.

Our feeling about pizza, a song, a religion, a book, certain kinds of cars, are influenced by experiences. The way a politician talks, or something you learn about them could make some people love them and others have the opposite feeling. Just like a movie, or a piece of chocolate!

We shouldn't be surprised our politics are different.

There are billionaires that are very liberal on social issues (think George Soros) and there are billionaires that are very conservative on social issues (think the Koch brothers). There are billionaires that support the Democrats (like Warren Buffett) and billionaires that support the Republicans (say, Sheldon Adelson). You have billionaires that are a little more liberal but like Republicans (Peter Thiel) and billionaires that are a little more conservative but like Democrats (say Warren Buffett, Steve Ballmer). There are billionaires that like politics such as Meg Whitman, Mark Cuban, Donald Trump, Oprah Winfrey and Michael Bloomberg. But for all the media coverage to any and all of them most billionaires are in the shadows of politics. Most corporate types are going to play it close to the vest—support both sides. If you have a lot of money and business at stake you don't want to upset one side or the other; you want them both to be friends.

And so it goes with the political circle. You can put liberals and conservatives on separate sides and then define the top and bottom a certain way—say establishment vs anti-establishment. However, you are going to find establishment Democrats and Republicans that are passionate about certain social issues. And, you are going to find anti-establishment citizens that aren't as concerned about social issues.

A New Establishment

The statistics demonstrate reason for optimism. Particularly in the last 10 years the trend is accelerating of voters identifying as "independent," as opposed to one party or the other. In 2015, Gallup found 42% of survey respondents chose independent (29% Democrat, 26% Republican).[88] And, as of December 2017, independent identification had further enlarged, to 46% (27,25).[89]

But so many times in life things get better and better and better… or worse and worse and worse… before they change the other direction.

Despite a changing desire among voters the same 2 parties continue to dominate. The irony is that the big, powerful parties might be ready to get even bigger, and more dominant. These parties could go international?

They work hard to maintain their power. They co-opt movements. They fund both sides; and dip their hands in anything new—ensuring to leave nothing to chance in their power. Big roadblocks are up to prevent established interests from losing their political power. For example, ballot access laws that make it difficult for third party candidates to appear on the ballot. The committees and power structures of the House and Senate and the seniority rules.

The media too—the gatekeeper for corporate/banker establishment interests. The media wants to ruin any chance of real change. Keep us complacent. Keep us divided. Keep real truths hidden as they protect the corporate/banker narrative. And you have the political party and party loyalists. They are spreading their own messages. Trying to influence people to their side. They spread false information. They rile people up. All designed to build and/or solidify their own support. Using the media, staging false issues.

New legislation does not reflect what the people want. How many more 1,500-page bills passed at 2 a.m. do we need?

**The dominate issue for a new political alignment is
breaking up the control of a self-serving
political establishment of elites.**

Once an insider himself, David Stockman proposes that a "countervailing power" must be established as those currently lacking power and influence

---

[88] http://content.gallup.com/origin/gallupinc/GallupSpaces/Production/Cms/POLL/6lfnhxwzy0qumyhgcnobdg.png

[89] http://news.gallup.com/poll/15370/party-affiliation.aspx

"become organized and unified." Stockman says, "the current left-right battle" is "preventing such an alliance from forming."[90]

The so-called "extremes" may have things in common.

It is not always explicit

What if certain economic reforms became the center point? There would even have to be very hard sacrifices even to come to agreement on economic improvements. However, in the grand scheme this may be a much better result and society for the broader population.

does a new party emerge in the middle of the two old parties? Or, does it emerge as a new left, or new right party? Or, do the issue dynamics shift to completely different issues allowing for a new look at the traditional spectrum.

Just Like That

What I do believe is that momentum will come out of nowhere for big changes. What is inevitable cannot be held back.

Just as the Declaration of Independence was a bold gong struck loudly and out of the blue to the powerful King George III[91], it is not out of the realm of possibility to, for all intents and purposes, wake up one day to see the United States heading in unforeseen directions. You cannot hold back inevitability.

An incredible shift is very possible.

The further the rubber band gets stretched, the more dramatically it snaps back. I believe the establishment is so determined to hold on to power with so much effort that it will indeed be able to. But eventually they are going to pull the rubber band too far and it will break. Or it will slip from their fingers and snap back. What that means is incredible change up and out of nowhere. Be prepared. It just might be coming.

The current signs of populist momentum by the people is being scapegoated/derided by establishment media,[92] but that laughing may not last.

Congress might just rather suddenly shift to the people.

Waitresses and truck drivers. Rappers. Literally.

All the money won't matter.

Corporations and lobbyists won't be able to stop the flow that might be coming.

---

[90] *The Great Deformation*, David A. Stockman. 2013.

[91] https://en.wikipedia.org/wiki/George_III_of_the_United_Kingdom

[92] https://www.politico.com/magazine/story/2018/01/14/trump-populism-history-216320

Be ever so careful. Because the bankers will be creating the new and the cool. And they will co-opt whatever they can. It will be when you see them kicking and screaming at someone. That is the movement that is too close to the vault… and aka. on the right track.

We need to expect more in America.

We need to aim higher. It won't take much. The smallest tweak in the percentage of people that go to the polls could have *huge* impacts.

Can we get government that is FOR the people, by the people? Is that the 4th branch of government? To create a government "of the people," "by the people" and "for the people" we need to shatter the traditional political spectrum. This will enable more conversation—deeper, tougher dialogue—which will continue to deliver on the promise of the American dream.[93]

We do not all sit along a line from far left to far right. We are all, each of us, a lot more independent and unique than such classification. When we shatter viewing politics along a line, embrace the "quantum politics" mindset of the "political circle" it will open our political world to a lot more people, and potential.

We need to shatter the old Washington DC establishment, break the tired messaging of a loud-mouth media and get some fresh energy. Never doubt that we are smart enough to handle some real innovation. Never fear voting for something completely different. If we try sometimes, we might find it's really what we need.

In a free and dynamic society there could be unprecedented challenges and unknown difficulties ahead. At the same time, all of us have so much unique potential to contribute to an awesome future of continued ingenious inventions and positive development.

We need to work together. It will take all of us. Passionate radicals; calm, collected facilitators. Liberals, conservatives. Moderates—those that can bridge divides; and especially those that can facilitate by listening to all perspectives, even extremes. The variations from person to person are what will make the best future possible.

Along one circle, together, appreciating the value we all bring. A journey to this point. And a journey that will keep on going.

Through deeper dialogue, aimed at win-win-win solutions we can bring out the best in our wide-ranging political viewpoints and change politics forever. The best is yet to come. The best conversations. The best society. The best solutions.

I have always felt it all starts with you.

And that culture is contagious.

If you don't make a change don't expect others to. And when you do change, expect to see it popping up more around you.

---

[93] https://youtu.be/5J6jAC6XxAI?t=12m45s

ABOUT THE AUTHOR

Marcus Bowman has two previous published books, *Links Poetry* and *Financial Fair Hope*. The latter on reforming our economic system with a title that is a play on words for his latest hometown.

Marcus moved to Fairhope, Alabama in 2012 following 12 years in Washington, DC where he earned a Master of Public Policy (MPP). In the nation's capital Marcus worked for a Japanese owned company researching federal legislation and political developments.

Marcus earned a B.S. in Finance with a minor in Economics from Iowa State University after growing up in the suburbs of Chicago, Illinois. In 2016, Marcus was blessed with his first and only child.